Successful Collaboration in Healthcare

A Guide for Physicians, Nurses and Clinical Documentation Specialists

Colleen Stukenberg
MSN, RN, CMSRN, CCDS

CRC Press
Taylor & Francis Group
Boca Raton London New York

CRC Press is an imprint of the
Taylor & Francis Group, an **informa** business
A PRODUCTIVITY PRESS BOOK

Productivity Press
Taylor & Francis Group
270 Madison Avenue
New York, NY 10016

Printed in the United States of America on acid-free paper
10 9 8 7 6 5 4 3 2 1

International Standard Book Number: 978-1-4398-1292-1 (Hardback)

Library of Congress Cataloging-in-Publication Data

Stukenberg, Colleen.
Successful collaboration in healthcare : a guide for physicians, nurses and clinical documentation specialists / Colleen Stukenberg.
p. ; cm.
Includes bibliographical references and index.
ISBN 978-1-4398-1292-1 (alk. paper)
1. Medical record personnel. 2. Hospitals--Case management services. 3. Medical cooperation. I. Title.
[DNLM: 1. Forms and Records Control--organization & administration. 2. Case Management--organization & administration. 3. Cooperative Behavior. 4. Documentation--economics. 5. Interprofessional Relations. 6. Medical Records Systems, Computerized. W 80 S934s 2010]

RA976.5.S78 2010
610.285--dc22 2009039136

Successful Collaboration in Healthcare

A Guide for Physicians, Nurses and Clinical Documentation Specialists

Contents

Preface

The creation of this book was initially vague because I did not have a definite emphasis. However, when I was encouraged to write something I was passionate about, the focus became clear. I frequently have been asked by colleagues, friends, and family what I do at work. Because the clinical documentation specialist (CDS) role is still new, I believed a book might help others understand the role better, as well as its relationship to other roles in healthcare. With my background in case management and nursing, I was able to apply various pieces to outline the CDS role.

THE JOURNEY: FROM BEDSIDE NURSE TO CDS

Beginning at the Bedside

To understand how healthcare collaboration can be successful, I will start with my professional journey that began more than 20 years ago. My first nursing role was a part-time evening charge nurse in a hospital skilled nursing unit. Because the unit was new and did not require multiple staff, I learned early to know who my resources were. This included a certified nursing assistant who had previously worked in another area of the hospital and knew where I could find anything I might need during my shift, including ordering tests and obtaining supplies. In addition, I counted heavily on the evening nursing supervisors for policies, procedures, clinical questions, and advice. As I grew professionally, I wanted to increase my clinical experience and began working on a medical-surgical-orthopedic unit as a staff nurse and an evening charge nurse. This provided me a strong clinical base. As my knowledge increased so did my desire for an expanded challenge. I decided to spread my wings and began working in an intensive care unit (ICU) to broaden my knowledge. Although this move opened up an entire world of exciting experiences, it was not to be my final calling.

Minimum Data Sets Care Coordinator Role

My next phase took me back to the hospital skilled nursing unit as a staff nurse and minimum data sets (MDS) care coordinator. The MDS coordinator role was a nursing position that completed the required MDS paperwork for the federal government in a skilled nursing unit. Although this role did not seem to be a normal transition following the world of intensive care, there was a purpose behind this unusual change in my career. My career change occurred before the inception of the prospective payment system (PPS) for skilled nursing units with the Balanced Budget Act of 1997. Instead of skilled nursing units being paid by Medicare for reasonable costs, they would be paid per diem following the PPS. This payment would cover ancillary services, nursing care, and capital costs. In addition, this per diem rate would include coverage for the majority of services given to patients in a skilled nursing unit with a few exceptions, such as certain predetermined outpatient procedures, computerized axial tomography (CT) scans, and magnetic resonance imaging (MRIs). Instead of being able to charge separately for lab tests, basic x-rays, therapies, and other services, most were bundled in this payment. This concept of payment was a significant change for these skilled facilities because they needed to have a thorough understanding of how the payment was determined and what influenced it. The payment was determined by the patient's clinical condition and the services he or she received within a specific period as defined by the MDS manual. This information would be entered into the MDS form, which would place the patient into a specific category called a resource utilization group (RUG). For example, if the patient received more than 500 minutes of physical therapy 5 days a week, it would place the patient in one RUG category. If the patient received intravenous antibiotic therapy and required specific nursing care, he or she would be placed in a different RUG category. Each RUG category correlated to a rate that would be used as the multiplier to determine the per diem rate for the patient for a set period. Because this payment RUG was determined by the information entered in the MDS, the MDS care coordinator played a vital role in obtaining the accurate information from the patient, reviewing the medical record, and entering the information into the MDS form. The role required an intense understanding of the MDS manual, detailed chart reviews, and accurate documentation of the patient's corresponding information.

Implementing the transition to PPS was not as simple as understanding the MDS role. Many hours went into in-depth research of understanding the PPS system, RUGs, MDS, and care coordination. In addition, computerized documentation was initiated in the skilled nursing unit to reflect the required verbiage of the MDS. Staff training was implemented regarding the description of terms used in the MDS. This helped staff to understand the documentation required to correspond with the MDS wording. Because the terms "limited" assist or "extensive" assist had specific descriptions in the MDS manual, staff were trained to understand how they applied in the documentation of patient care. In addition, because the MDS form was multidisciplinary, the care coordinator collaborated with workers in other disciplines, such as the dietician, physical therapist, occupational therapist, and activity director, to complete the form. Weekly team meetings with staff from each discipline brought together everyone's experience and education for the benefit of the patient. This group collaboration with staff, understanding the link between the clinical and financial aspects of the MDS, and being able to correlate it to patient care and government regulations seemed to be an entirely different perspective of nursing than what I originally understood. Although I did not realize it at the time, the change to this role was a turning point in my career.

Health Case Manager

The next phase of my journey was a more obvious transition as I took a position in the acute care side of the hospital as a health case manager. This provided an avenue for me to combine my knowledge as an MDS care coordinator with my clinical background of medical, surgical, orthopedic, and intensive care nursing into a more holistic view of case management. I combined clinical, social, financial, quality, and regulatory aspects into the role. I had past experience with the role of quality monitoring in the ICU and skilled nursing facility with data collection, monitoring for patterns, trends, and outcomes, and implementing changes through staff education. Although many clinical, social, financial, quality, and regulatory aspects changed over the years, applying the holistic view did not. In addition, the case management role provided another opportunity for my professional growth, as this position was a physician-based case management model. Although I had worked with physicians before as a staff nurse, I began to see healthcare from the physician's perspective. When I was still the nurse, I began to see how various disciplines interacted differently. Physicians appeared to look at patients from a more factual and data-driven perspective. What were the vital signs? What were the lab results? What were the test results? The focus was not how the information was obtained or what the process was but what were the outcomes or results. Although the physicians did consider the patient as a person, they tended to keep a more focused approach because hospital patient rounds were only a part of their complex day. The nurse was more involved with the "how-to" assignments and processes of getting the work done. In addition, the nurse focused intensely on his or her patient group during an 8- or 12-hour shift; however, the nurse was able to go home when the shift was over. Although a nurse did not necessarily forget about the work, he or she could hand off patient care responsibilities to the oncoming nurse. In contrast, the physician may be called multiple times during the 24-hour period about this patient and others while handling his or her office workload, meetings, and other crises. This is not to say one role is more important than another, but each has different foci and responsibilities. Another contrast was how information was interpreted differently between physicians and nurses. A physician would write an order at 6:00 PM to "Increase furosemide to 60 mg daily." Although the physician may think this is a clear order, the nurse may question whether the physician wants the medication increased today (because the patient already had 40 mg of furosemide at 8:00 AM) or with the next morning dose. This may seem simple, but it demonstrates how two people can interpret the same information differently. In addition, as I spent more time on rounds with physicians, I began to see how miscommunication and frustration could occur from both nursing and physician perspectives. Just as the unit nurse may not see the challenges the physician faces in balancing his or her office and hospital worlds, the physician may not understand the complexity of completing orders and taking care of one patient while assuming the care of four or five other patients, along with admissions, discharges, and other situations that arise throughout a shift. Seeing both sides of the fence enlightened me as I continued my career journey.

Clinical Development Specialist

The next phase of my career had a different emphasis as my pathway shifted to nursing staff development. Although this did not seem to be a branch off my earlier paths, it offered an opportunity to advance my education and understand nursing and growth from a different perspective. The clinical development specialist role focused on mentoring new and current nurses through their professional careers. Obtaining my master's degree in nursing education and developing my own professional career was challenging, but reaching out to help others develop shone another light on my professional path. I needed to understand my own growth and development and where I was in the continuum of life before I could begin to understand how to help others build their paths. Although I did not continue teaching new nurses as a professional role, I had a greater understanding of others' behaviors and thought processes depending on where they were in their own careers. Was this a novice person just starting out, or had this person become adept in his or her field? This awareness helped me realize that not everyone is at the same career stage at the same time. Nor does everyone reach the same levels at the same pace. In addition, people communicate and learn differently. To help others, one needs to have an awareness of different learning styles and communication behaviors. Again, this part of my career provided another building block to my future as I took on a new endeavor.

Clinical Documentation Management Professional

During the clinical development specialist role, I was asked to pilot a clinical documentation role that focused on physician's documentation. The accuracy of physician documentation was becoming a new initiative in healthcare as positions were created to assist physicians in the accuracy of their documentation and to demonstrate how documentation relates to the clinical picture of the patient, as well as having financial and quality impacts for an organization. This position allowed me to take pieces of my various earlier nursing roles and incorporate them into the clinical documentation management professional position. Within the first year, the program was determined to be a success, and the role was made permanent. Although this role will be explained in the following chapters, understanding my journey provides insight on how this role fits into healthcare collaboration. The purpose of this book is to provide a guide on how the clinical documentation management professional role (also known as a clinical documentation specialist) can successfully collaborate with physicians and nurses in healthcare. Although this book may not be applicable in all settings, it provides a guide to understanding the role. Use of the material should be at the reader's discretion, as it was designed to provide an understanding of the role and not absolute criteria.

Acknowledgments

Although many people provided support while I wrote this book, I must first acknowledge God, who guides me in all I do. I also thank my husband Mike, children Ryan and Nathan, and my family, colleagues, and friends who continue to support me. When I finished my master's degree in nursing, we all thought I had reached my goal. However, no sooner had I accomplished that feat, I was given the challenge to write this book. Special thanks go to Tammy Gorenyuk and Kris Mednansky, who both encouraged me to accept this challenge, and to Lisa Carey and Stacey Deneen, who provided insight into my writing. Although I could list many other people to personally thank, I would not want to forget anyone. I have never considered myself a writer; however, I feel I was given a purpose.

1

Introduction

Keeping current in today's ever-changing healthcare world can be challenging for providers, staff, and organizations. Healthcare is not maintained in a bubble but is affected by many aspects, including technology, regulations, and reimbursement. These are just some areas about which healthcare workers must stay abreast. Technology seems to expand faster than the average person can comprehend. Computers, e-mails, cell phones, text messaging, and electronic imaging are examples of the way technology impacts our lives. No sooner do we purchase a computer system than it is replaced by something newer and more advanced. In addition, technology has affected how we communicate. No longer is it necessary to have face-to-face meetings when we can "meet" in a virtual setting. This ability has allowed communication to occur across various time zones without the need for travel, as well as for quicker dissemination of information and for decisions to be made more rapidly. In addition to the changes in technology, healthcare regulations and reimbursement are frequently adjusted or amended. Considering technology adds to the ability to modify and distribute these changes, keeping current is even more crucial. Physicians, nurses, and case managers are challenged by these changes. Clinicians not only need to stay abreast of medical and scientific aspects of healthcare, they also must understand and keep current of how technology and regulations affect their roles. How does an electronic record affect data entry and chart documentation? How do regulations such as the Health Insurance Portability and Accountability Act of 1996 (HIPAA) affect these clinical roles as they need to share information while maintaining compliance? How do physicians, nurses, and case managers keep current with government regulations and institute changes into their workflows? These are just some of the questions one may ask when considering various changes in healthcare. However, clinicians should not think they are alone in this challenge. Understanding different healthcare roles and how they intertwine can help the process of keeping current with change. Knowing, or at least partially understanding, others' roles can provide a resource for one's own role regarding whom to go to with questions and ideas. As clinicians in various roles collaborate, they can successfully overcome the challenges found in healthcare's dynamic setting. Collaboration provides an opportunity for people in various disciplines to work together to create positive outcomes.

Many different types of healthcare providers, including physicians, nurses, and case managers, can build an alliance that affects safe, quality patient care and impacts finances positively through a variety of opportunities. Nurses can work in various roles with physicians to provide quality care while meeting the requirements of federal and state governing bodies and considering the financial impacts to their organization. These nursing positions may include the direct patient caregiver, the charge or team leader nurse, the case manager, and the clinical documentation specialist (CDS), a newly emerging role. Regulating and financial impacts may include recovery audit contractors (RACs), present on admission (POA), healthcare-acquired conditions (HACs), diagnosis-related groups (DRGs), and value-based purchasing (VBP).

Building this alliance among healthcare workers requires more than people doing their jobs. This partnership involves collaborating in a positive manner to achieve a goal or outcome. The concept of working as a team is not new. We were taught to get along with each other as children. We were told to get along with our siblings, friends, teammates, and even possibly our enemies. We may have been taught by a good teacher or learned by trial and error how to work together. The saying *two heads are better than one* supports working together. How often have we struggled to fix something or learn a new process but are not successful until we work together with someone else?

To understand how workers in various healthcare roles can collaborate to become an effective team, one must first understand what constitutes good collaboration. Communication is the basis for collaboration. Effective communication is built on trust and respect. In addition, understanding another's roles from his or her perspective facilitates communication. After one has an understanding of communication, one can then apply that learning to improve quality and understand the financial aspects of healthcare. Understanding how communication links the various healthcare roles helps one to understand how he or she can impact these outcomes.

As mentioned previously, there are many types of healthcare roles: physicians, nurses, case managers, and CDSs. Each discipline may carry its own specialty, for example, physicians being internal medicine physicians, pediatricians, surgeons, and cardiologists. Nurses may vary depending on units or specialties, such as medical, surgical, orthopedic, critical care, emergency, obstetrics, or hospice nurses, or in roles such as team leader, staff nurse, charge nurse, or director. Case managers may be designated by different focuses such as hospital, disease management, worker's compensation, and community-based case managers. To confuse matters more, some organizations may call one discipline one name, whereas another organization calls the same role or position another name. Although organizations may use different names or titles for various roles, it is the crux of the role that matters. What are the functions of the role? What are the credentials? What is the experience? How is the information applied? What is the process? These are aspects to consider when deciding who is doing what job. Finally, after understanding the roles and potential impacts, one can see how the process potentially fits together in a variety of situations. Being able to apply information is crucial to understanding how healthcare collaboration can be successful.

This book will provide a guide to understanding the clinical documentation role, including how it relates to nurse and physician roles. Communication of physicians, nurses, and CDSs in the hospital setting will be described as it relates to collaboration. Understanding aspects of communication is the beginning of collaboration. In addition, understanding and applying communication tools such as SBAR (*s*ituation, *b*ackground, *a*ssessment, and *r*ecommendation) will be described. Another aspect of collaboration is understanding how people in different roles view information through three types of knowledge: person, patient, and case.

After understanding communication, next comes the ability to understand how quality and financial components influence the roles of physicians, nurses, and CDSs. Surprisingly to some, quality and financial aspects can overlap in healthcare. Understanding terms that relate to quality and finances, such as length of stay (LOS), DRG, POA, and HAC, helps us begin to fit together the pieces of the puzzle. Explanation and application of these terms provide additional opportunities for comprehension. However, the links do not end here, as other pieces, including VBP and public reporting of information, form part of the larger picture. Then, just when one is able to complete the puzzle, the government revamps the picture to include RACs.

As the complexity of healthcare has grown beyond understanding the clinical and technical areas of taking care of patients to include financial and quality concerns, the CDS role has emerged and is explained in greater detail in Chapter 4. This role is more than someone policing physician documentation. This role combines clinical areas with coding and regulatory concerns. It has grown as many hospitals have made it a permanent program in their organizations. In addition, vendors also include this documentation role in their computerized systems. Although computerized systems may help with the technical components, understanding the role and the process is crucial for the success of the CDS position. In Chapter 4 the role is further explained as the CDS process is highlighted. In addition, the five reasons to query a physician are addressed. According to the American Health Information Management Association (AHIMA), these include "legibility," "completeness," "clarity," "consistency," and "precision."

Understanding why to query a physician helps complete the clinical picture. Just as one cannot judge a book by a cover, one cannot "see" the true clinical picture of the patient until the picture is described completely, clearly, and accurately. For example, the book may be titled *Pneumonia*, but one does not know what the book is truly about unless it is further described. Just as the title is not complete, a patient's diagnosis of pneumonia does not adequately describe the patient. The pneumonia should be further detailed, including the type, organism, comorbid conditions, and other supporting information.

The CDS role does not end with documentation. Data collection helps support how the role fits into quality and financial aspects of healthcare. In addition, the role is not for everyone. It requires the right mix of education, experience, and communication skills. Education and training are vital for the CDS role; however, this education does not end with the CDS. It must be expanded to include physicians and nurses because the team needs to understand how they fit together. Education of the role is an ongoing process as healthcare continues to experience changes in technology, regulations, and clinical information. Understanding the process of change as it relates to education can facilitate the process.

Although this guide, including figures, tools, and scenarios, was designed to cover the various aspects of the CDS role and healthcare collaboration with physicians and nurses, the opportunities for change and growth continue to be part of healthcare. Keeping current with these changes and incorporating them into an organization's existing system and processes are not only part of today but also of the future.

2

Building Trust and Communication

Communication sounds like a simple task that should occur naturally. However, this natural art does not come easily for everyone. In addition, the same can be said for collaboration through communication. Whereas some people appear to work together and communicate easily, others require more deliberate efforts. Building this collaborating alliance through teamwork requires energy. Successful collaboration requires us to have self-awareness. We need to know our strengths and weaknesses and the potential impact they have on others. In addition, we need to know and understand our communication style. Self-awareness of our communication style and behavior is an important step in understanding how we present ourselves to others. To understand how people communicate, we must understand some of the different communication styles.

COMMUNICATION STYLES

There are many styles of communication that one may observe when interacting with different personality types. The topic of communication styles could be a book in itself; however, for basic purposes the main four types focus on behaviors of *aggressiveness*, *passive-aggressiveness*, *passiveness*, and *assertiveness*. These styles can build positive collaboration or break down communication through negativity. Understanding the differences in these styles can provide a basis for learning how to communicate effectively.

Aggressiveness

Aggressiveness has a negative connotation and may be described by words such as "hostility," "belligerence," and "forcefulness" (Microsoft Encarta, 2006). The aggressive person may display an angry expression, including a stern stance and a brazen voice that says he or she does not care about the results as long as the person gets what he or she wants. The person may have an uncompromising behavior and focuses on his or her own needs instead of considering others. The aggressiveness may come in the form of an outburst, leaving the remaining spectators startled and astounded. The aggressive communicator may shout, "I want it fixed, and I want it fixed now! I don't really care how it is done—just do it or else!" Although this outburst may seem extreme, the aggressive behavior makes the person's point known in a controlling manner. This bullying behavior does not promote professionalism but rather adds tension to the environment. People may be fearful of the person's aggressive behavior to the point they do not want to speak with him or her and further avoid any interactions. This avoidance impedes future conversation because people may decide it is easier to avoid the person than deal with the aggressive behavior.

Passive-Aggressiveness

Avoidance may also be seen when communicating with a person who is *passive-aggressive.* The passive-aggressive style is demonstrated by the person does not wish to communicate directly with another. Instead of speaking with the person, the passive-aggressive communicator chooses to interact indirectly. He or she manipulates by avoiding confrontational issues. The passive-aggressive communicator may leave a message with someone else to give to the person he or she is avoiding to keep from speaking with the individual in person. This behavior may be seen with someone who is fearful of another person's reaction but still wants to achieve his or her own result. Passive-aggressive behavior may also be seen when a person sabotages another's work or idea by outwardly appearing as if he or she is going to support the changes or ideas but in reality does not follow through with his or her commitments. An example would be if the person agrees that a change to a work form is a good idea but later tells others he or she does not plan to use it. Or the person may even tell others not to use the form but denies what he or she said if asked. The passive-aggressive person does not want to deal with conflict directly but would prefer to use negative behaviors such as gossiping to get what he or she wants or to express him- or herself (Zeiler, 2008). This type of behavior may not be recognized as easily as the aggressive person's behavior because others may not realize it is happening immediately. However, as the passive-aggressive behavior is demonstrated in a variety of settings and situations, others may see the pattern and realize this person chooses to avoid a situation directly. Instead, he or she allows others to deal with the consequences of his or her actions in these difficult situations.

Passiveness

Passiveness may initially be seen in passive-aggressive behavior, but the passive person tends to be more timid and puts other's feelings, needs, or desires first. This person wants to keep peace and will avoid confrontations. He or she will not "stir the waters" when interacting with others. He or she may agree with everyone else regardless of his or her own thoughts or opinions. Different from the passive-aggressive person, the passive person will not comment or express his or her opinion. His or her behavior focuses so much on what others want that the person may not even ask or state what he or she wants. If the passive person does express his or her own opinion, he or she does it in a safe environment. If the response is negative, the passive person may not pursue any further communication or requests. On a continuum, passive communication may be at one end of the spectrum and aggressive communication at the opposite end. When a passive person and an aggressive person interact, negative results may exacerbate each other's communication style. The passive person becomes more withdrawn, and the aggressive person becomes more forceful. Passiveness may not initially be considered a negative attribute; however, because the passive person is not able to express him- or herself, the results may be negative.

Assertiveness

A balance of the different aspects of communication styles may be seen in the assertive style. Although the assertive person is not afraid to express him- or herself as a passive person may be, he or she is neither hostile nor belligerent as an aggressive person. *Assertiveness* is characterized by honest, open communication in a nonthreatening manner. Microsoft Encarta (2006) defines assertive as being "confident in stating a position or claim." People who are assertive may speak using facts with a nondefensive approach. They take ownership for their own thoughts and do not put the blame on others. Although they are confident and know what they want, they also have the ability to listen to others. This demonstrates a safe environment and respect for both parties. Assertiveness represents a positive communication style. Being assertive does not mean one knows all of the answers or is always right. Being honest and admitting one does not know the answer promotes positive interaction. This person acknowledges he or she does not understand a concept or have the answer but is willing to research the information, use available resources, or find out who may help in the situation. This type of behavior promotes honest communication.

Assertive communication is not just for people in positions of leadership; it can also be used by nurses, physicians, and clinical documentation specialists as they communicate information with each other. When we consider the differences in communication styles, we may picture someone who has characteristics of a certain style. However, we should remember who is a role model for the assertive style so we can keep this picture in our mind when we are communicating with others. Clear, honest, confident, and nonthreatening communication can provide an effective medium for sharing information and promoting collaboration.

ASPECTS OF COMMUNICATION

In addition to being assertive when communicating with others, one should look for the "win-win" situation when possible. It is not a matter of "us against them" or "who's right and who's wrong." Part of communication is sharing information and not pointing fingers. Positive communication entails listening and considering different perspectives, presenting information clearly and in a nonthreatening manner, and realizing that although one may be confident with his or her ideas, there may be a better solution or idea. When considering different solutions, the involved parties should consider the main goals and desired outcomes. Where do these overlap? What are the common areas the parties are focusing on?

What areas cannot be changed because of regulations or safety considerations? What areas are desires but are not required? For example, everyone may want a million-dollar budget for his or her department; however, if this is not possible, one should determine what the mandatory, regulatory, or safety needs are. What are the "must haves" versus the "want to haves?" Working together to achieve a common goal and desired outcomes supports the win-win situation.

Achieving the win-win outcome may seem to be a simple task, but it does not always occur. Even in a work setting, negativity can be displayed in aggressive or passive-aggressive behaviors. An example may be demonstrated when a committee discusses changes in an organization. The group may attempt to look for the win-win situation, but all parties do not agree on the goals or outcomes. Although no one is directly aggressive in the meeting, when it is over, the noise starts as disgruntled parties express their opinions. This impedes productivity, as the conversations are not expressed with the appropriate people who need to hear the information. Instead, the discussion occurs where or when others who are not concerned may hear. Although the information may reach the intended group, the message may be completely distorted. This concept of error when passing along information is similar to the childhood game of "telephone" or "whisper down the alley." One person starts the message and whispers it to his or her neighbor who whispers it to his or her neighbor until it goes around the circle and reaches the person who started the message. By the time it reaches the original person, it is not only inaccurate, it is also so distorted that the message does not even make sense. This can occur when communication does not occur directly between all parties.

COMMUNICATION AND TRUST

Aggressive and passive-aggressive communication does not promote trust. Although one may argue that an assertive person is not always trustful either, the assertive person demonstrates respect. Trust and respect are not equivalent, but they are two positive aspects when communicating. How does one earn trust? One could say a person needs to respect the other person to trust him or her or vice versa. Some characteristics that promote trust are knowledge, accuracy, and follow-through. If someone falls short in any of these areas, trust may not develop. One may be very knowledgeable in his or her field or career but does not always accurately present information, thoughts, or ideas. In addition, the person may not follow up on requests or projects. An example would be if the person is an expert in critical care nursing but does not give the correct lab results or clinical picture of the patient. Or the person may give the correct clinical picture but does not follow up by calling the physician with an update as requested. In contrast, the person may follow through with the projects, but the information presented is inaccurate or not current. This can happen when a person receives a request for a report from a committee. The person presents the report as requested, but the information is not accurate or current. These situations do not establish trust among the others.

EMOTIONAL MATURITY

Another aspect of communication is emotional maturity. This incorporates understanding and controlling one's own expressions, thoughts, and behaviors while identifying and acknowledging others (Lindeke and Sieckert, 2008). Emotional maturity may be demonstrated by expressing oneself in a sensible manner. This level of maturity does not end once achieved. One cannot put it on a shelf and expect these qualities to fall into place whenever he or she communicates with others. Without a conscious effort to take control of one's maturity, a person's innate characteristics may overtake the learned ones. This may be seen in a highly stressful situation creating conflict. Conflict can cause stress, and stress can add to conflict. This snowball effect may be seen as tension escalates. A person's ability to control his or her behavior and language is superseded by the tension and frustration of the environment. The person loses control of his or her emotional self. This may come in the form of yelling, making unrealistic demands, or making an inaccurate assumption of cause and effect.

An example of emotional immaturity may be demonstrated when a person wants a chest radiograph report "now" that has not even been done or when a person assumes the reason the radiograph was not done is because the computer system to order the test is outdated. When the person complains, "I never get my test reports when I need them" or "Nothing works right around here," he or she is making generalized statements that are not necessarily true. However, an emotionally mature person does not make a generalized outburst but instead is able to analyze the situation. The person realizes after speaking with the staff nurse he or she cannot get a report on a chest radiograph "now" that has not even been done. It would also be more accurate to state the person wants the chest radiograph *done* now. In addition, complaining that the computer system is outdated may be an incorrect assumption if the real reason the radiograph was not done was because the x-ray room was not available at the time the test was ordered.

Although many of us have been in tense situations where time is crucial for patient outcomes, expressing negative comments and rudeness does not alleviate the stressful situation. Instead, this emotional outburst may escalate the stress of the situation. Controlling one's own emotional behavior is not only important for the sender but also the receiver of the message. How one responds can add fuel to the fire or extinguish the flames. If the person does complain, "I never get my test reports when I need them," the responder should not argue back about the accuracy of the statement. Maybe this statement was prompted because the patient may be demonstrating signs of acute pulmonary edema with congestive heart failure (CHF) and the physician wanted a chest radiograph to help diagnose the condition. Patient care should be the priority in this situation and not the general statement of not getting reports. Instead, the focus should be on what can be done to get the patient radiograph and treatment he or she needs. After the patient's care has been addressed, the situation can be examined to determine whether processes are in place for emergent situations. In addition, after analyzing the situation and looking at potential processes, communicating results of the analyses and formulating a process to help prevent the issue in the future can help clear up the situation.

COMMUNICATION ASSESSMENT

Although communicating with emotional maturity may be the desire, what happens when a person has attempted to communicate effectively but another person still responds aggressively or does not respond at all? These two frustrating situations can impede further communication. First, one should go back to the initial lesson of knowing one's own communication style. Assess how the sender approached the receiver. One may need to ask an objective party what he or she observed. What did the objective person hear during the conversation? What was the tone? How did the sender address the receiver? How did the receiver respond? This may be difficult because a productive solution requires honest, constructive criticism by the third party. In addition, the sender must be willing to listen to the assessment. This step is not about who is right or wrong but how the sender expressed his or her message. After hearing this analysis, one can determine what he or she could have done differently. Next, one should consider the environment in which the communication took place. Was it in an appropriate setting? Should the conversation happen privately or in a less public area? Was the tension of the environment appropriate for the timing of the conversation? Asking about a scheduling conflict with an employee during an emergent patient situation such as a cardiac arrest is obviously not appropriate timing.

If the assessment was that the sender's message and situation were appropriate, then one should evaluate the response of the receiver. Ask the third party how he or she perceived the receiver's response. How one interprets the response may be different than what actually occurred. This can happen when the two people have had past difficulties with communication. One or both may feel the other did not respond properly; however, to the objective observer, the conversation may have been appropriate. If the receiver did respond aggressively or ignore the communication, then the sender needs to determine his or her best response. The response should focus primarily on patient safety. If the message is crucial to the safety of the patient, then the sender needs to make sure the appropriate person receives the communication. If one has attempted to communicate but is unsuccessful, he or she should follow the organization's chain of command to get the information to the appropriate person. However, when the message can wait or be delivered in another method, the sender should consider his or her own response to the situation. Storming off with a rebuttal or negative retort demonstrates the inability of that person in controlling his or her behavior. Attempting to understand the receiver's perspective may be more beneficial. Listening is an important aspect of attempting to understand another's viewpoint. The receiver may have information that the sender was not aware of. Keeping an open mind and being nonjudgmental may be vital in understanding the other's perspective. In addition, being positive and stating facts clearly are constructive approaches in conveying information. However, there are some circumstances when the sender may have to calmly take a deep breath and continue with his or her work. This is not about ignoring the conversation but realizing there are times when it is advantageous not to contribute to a potentially hostile situation. After assessing the circumstances, one should discuss the situation with the appropriate person outlined in the organization's policy.

CODE OF CONDUCT

Communication is not limited to affecting just the two communicating parties but can affect patient care. If there is a strain on communication as seen with aggressive or passive communication or emotional immaturity, the information required to take care of a patient may not be discussed adequately or in a timely manner. If a person is too afraid to speak to another provider about a patient's condition because he or she is fearful of being degraded or the receiver of the provider's outbursts, the patient may not receive the care he or she needs. If a staff member must call with a change in a patient's condition, but the receiver yells at the person, belittles the caller's input, or responds in other negative ways, the caller may avoid calling the person in the future. Or the caller may provide only minimal information so that he or she can get off the telephone quickly, avoiding a negative response. Even if the receiver does not make any unconstructive comments, the anticipation of fear from the caller may prevent the person from staying on the phone long enough to answer all of the questions, give a clear picture, or receive complete orders. Fear of inappropriate behaviors or conduct should not impede patient care.

Inappropriate behaviors have escalated to a level of awareness that is recognized by The Joint Commission. In 2009, two aspects of a new leadership standard speak to this issue. According to The Joint Commission, accredited organizations need to have a "code of conduct that defines acceptable and disruptive and inappropriate behaviors." In addition, the leaders need to "create and implement a process for managing disruptive and inappropriate behaviors" (The Joint Commission, EP 4 and EP 5, 2008). This heightened awareness of the effects of behaviors in healthcare supports the need for positive communication. No longer should it be acceptable to say that doing excellent work is good enough to ignore bad behaviors.

COMMUNICATION TEMPLATE

Even after using appropriate communication behaviors and establishing an assertive style, the ability to effectively communicate does not end here. The information needs to be presented clearly and accurately. Organizing the information helps present this information clearly. If someone conveys information in a disorganized ramble, the receiver may have to sort out a jumbled mess. The sender's words do not create a clear picture because they are not arranged with any sense of order. This muddled information should be presented in an organized format. One way to organize information is by writing down the information in a specific arrangement. The idea of organizing one's thoughts through writing is not a new concept but may not be obvious. How often in our daily lives do we organize our thoughts through lists or a structured method? We write a grocery list. We create a "things to do" list. We schedule our lives using a calendar or prioritize our work in a visual format. Whatever our method, we have decided that having our information structured helps us to stay organized. Likewise, a template can help structure our thoughts so information can be presented more clearly to the receiver. The communication template might include headings or captions of certain data or material that needs to be presented. These headings may include date, time, name or title, data, and outcomes. They should be arranged in a logical order that will help the flow of information. The type of communication template and headers will depend on the situation for which the communication template will be used. If the communication template is for a home project, it may look different than a tool used in a healthcare setting such as a hospital.

In healthcare, the transmission of information is not just about organization but also about knowledge, accuracy, and trust, as these are crucial for the patient's safety and care. When a nurse calls a physician with a change in a patient's condition, the physician has to be able to trust that the nurse is knowledgeable, giving accurate information, and will follow through with the plan of care. According to Iacono (2003), physicians want organized and factual information when communicating with nurses. For novice employees, using a communication template may be helpful; however, many experienced employees also can benefit from this tool. In fact, The Joint Commission Accreditation recognizes communication as a Hospital National Patient Safety Goal (2009). A communication template can be created that supports information needed for the safe handoff of a patient. The template provides the vital information needed for the next person to safely take care of the patient.

SBAR: SITUATION, BACKGROUND, ASSESSMENT, AND RECOMMENDATION

One communication template used in healthcare and supported by the Institute for Healthcare Improvement (IHI) is communicating using the acronym SBAR: *s*ituation, *b*ackground, *a*ssessment, and *r*ecommendation (IHI.org, n.d.). Each word is a heading in the communication tool that provides a prompt of important reminders when communicating. What is the *situation* that is being described to the person? What is the *background* or history of the situation? What is the communicator's *assessment* of the problem, issue, or concern? What may be some *recommendations* or ideas the communicator is thinking about? This tool can guide staff through the process of knowing what is needed when conveying information to another person. Imagine the difference of using SBAR versus not using SBAR. See Scenario 2.1.

Although both conversations end with the same orders, the second using SBAR provides a more complete, immediate picture for the physician. In the first scenario, if the physician would have not asked as many questions, he might have not discovered the patient had congestive heart failure. Not using a template such as SBAR may lead to incomplete information, inappropriate orders, frustration, wasted time, and poor outcomes. When the physician does not know the patient, which can happen when the on-call physician is contacted at 2:00 AM, the outcomes may be worse as frustration escalates.

In contrast, using SBAR provides a base from which to present information in a logical format. In addition, it promotes critical thinking for the nurse as he or she gathers information and goes through the thought process. Providing accurate and factual information in an orderly fashion promotes positive communication that can support trust. The logical format that SBAR uses can be applied to communication in many settings and among various healthcare workers. This concept can be used when a staff nurse gives an update to a physician, charge nurse, or case manager.

SCENARIO 2.1

I. Conversation without SBAR

Nurse: Dr. Roe, this is Miranda from 3 East at the hospital. I have a patient of Dr. Jans who is more short of breath this evening. His name is Mark Williams.

Physician: What was the patient admitted with?

Nurse: Well, he was admitted with pneumonia.

Physician: What are his vital signs? Has he been dyspneic with the pneumonia, or is this worse?

Nurse: It seems worse. His temperature is 99.7, pulse 98, respirations 28, and blood pressure 145/89.

Physician: Is he wheezing? Does he have a nebulizer ordered?

Nurse: He just had a nebulizer treatment an hour ago. He does not have any wheezes, but his lung sounds have bilateral crackles, and he has an oxygen saturation of 90% on 3 L/min. He also has IV fluids at 125 cc/h.

Physician: Does he have any other health history? What is his urine output?

Nurse: He has a history of congestive heart failure, and he has voided 100 cc in the past 8 hours.

Physician: Get a STAT chest x-ray and B-type natriuretic peptide (BNP CHF), and give furosemide 20 mg IV. Decrease his IV fluids to TKO (to keep vein open). Please call me with an update of his condition, the chest x-ray results, and his urine output from the furosemide within an hour.

Nurse: OK. I will get the STAT chest x-ray and BNP CHF, give furosemide 20 mg IV, decrease his IV fluids to TKO, and call with an update within an hour. Thanks.

II. Conversation Using SBAR

Nurse: Dr. Roe, this is Miranda on 3 East at the hospital. (**Situation**) I have a patient of Dr. Jans who seems more short of breath this evening. His name is Mark Williams. (**Background**) He was admitted with pneumonia 2 days ago and seemed to be doing better, but this evening he is complaining of being more dyspneic. He has a history of congestive heart failure. (**Assessment**) His lungs have bilateral crackles. He has an oxygen saturation of 90% on 3 L/min. He also has IV fluids at 125 cc/h and has only voided 100 cc in the past 8 hours. Neither his abdomen nor bladder feels distended. His vital signs are temperature of 99.7, pulse 98, respirations 28, and blood pressure 145/89. (**Recommendation**) I wonder if he needs his fluids adjusted.

Physician: It sounds like he is in failure from his CHF and extra IV fluids. Has he had a chest x-ray or lab work today?

Nurse: He had a complete blood count this morning but no chest x-ray since admission that only showed the pneumonia.

Physician: Get a STAT chest x-ray and BNP CHF, and give furosemide 20 mg IV. Decrease his IV fluids to TKO. Please call me with an update of his condition, the chest x-ray results, and his urine output from the furosemide within an hour.

Nurse: OK. I will get the STAT chest x-ray and BNP CHF, give furosemide 20 mg IV, decrease his IV fluids to TKO, and call with an update within an hour. Thanks.

KNOWLEDGE DIFFERENCES

Expectations of others may be a challenge with communication when people have a variety of backgrounds, knowledge bases, and experience. One may expect a person to know exactly what the other person wants. The person may not understand why the other gives additional information he or she does not feel important. This can be a challenge with communication. Various roles in healthcare may affect how we collaborate as people with different knowledge bases may focus on different viewpoints. Liaschenko and Fisher postulate and describe three aspects of knowledge as it relates to nursing: person, patient, and case (Stein-Parbury and Liaschenko, 2007). Person knowledge refers to the ability of knowing the person's being, including how the person lives and fits into his or her surrounding environment. Where does the patient live? How does the patient get his or her medications? Who is available to support the patient? Patient knowledge refers to a patient's comprehension and familiarity of his or her disease and how he or she reacts to treatment. What does the patient know about his or her disease process? How long has the patient had the condition? Is the patient compliant with treatment when he or she is at home? Both person and patient knowledge require communication with the patient. In comparison, case knowledge focuses on the technical and methodical aspects of the person's disease and treatment. Case knowledge emphasizes the scientifically objective information of a disease. What does the patient's chest x-ray show? What are the patient's lab results? What is the patient's oxygen saturation? This information can be ascertained while reviewing and applying clinical knowledge without potentially even seeing the patient.

Whereas nurses may focus more on the person and patient knowledge bases, physicians may concentrate on the case knowledge. This difference in knowledge base may cause some disruption when nurses and physicians attempt to communicate about a patient's condition. Although all three aspects may be important when considering the patient's plan of care, the person considering one set of knowledge may not think the other set of knowledge is as important. For example, when a patient is admitted with pneumonia, both the physician and nurse may be concerned with the patient's lung sounds and administering appropriate antibiotics. However, the physician may be more interested in the white blood count (WBC) and sputum culture results, whereas the nurse may be concerned about the tolerance of activity. Whereas the physician may want to know the oxygen saturation is 91% on 2 liters of oxygen, the nurse may interject that the patient cannot get up to the chair without being dyspneic. In addition, the nurse may be concerned because the patient reports she has two young grandchildren she baby-sits and is fearful of them getting pneumonia from her. Although the physician and nurse may focus on different aspects, their ability to collaborate for the benefit of the patient should not be affected. When one considers the holistic perspective, the patient's WBC count, sputum culture, oxygen saturation, activity tolerance, and fears are all areas to consider when working as a team for the benefit of positive patient outcomes. Being able to integrate all three levels of knowledge gives a clearer picture of the patient, the response to his or her care, and future treatment plans.

Understanding and respecting different viewpoints can improve the ability to communicate and work together. Even among various nursing roles, one may have different perspectives of a situation. The nurse who is the direct patient caregiver may focus on the patient's assessment, the initiation of intravenous therapy, and supplemental oxygen. The charge nurse or team leader may be concerned with chart orders, following up with lab and x-ray results, and staffing issues. The nurse as a case manager reviews the patient's condition and treatment plan according to approved criteria, while also considering potential discharge plans and needs (see Chapter 3). No one role is more important than another—they all are part of taking care of the patient from various angles. Effective group collaboration in this setting can embrace professionalism (Lindeke and Sieckert, 2008).

WORKING TOGETHER

The different foci of knowledge can create different expectations and challenges. Attempting to understand another's point of view is helpful for effective communication. In addition, both parties need to determine the goals or outcomes of the situation. They need to realize that working together is important in reaching these goals. Standards of practice or evidence-based practice may help to align parties. Working together for the common goal allows all parties to pool their resources and enhance efficiency. In contrast, working independently may waste time and resources, as each person works toward the goal without the other person's contribution.

In Figure 2.1, for example, one can see Persons 1, 2, and 3 are all working toward the same goal. However, because there are barriers, such as each person receiving instructions from a different person or working in separate environments, the three persons may duplicate efforts, thus wasting time and resources. In addition, even if the barriers were removed, the people work toward the goal independently because their lines of communication do not cross. If the barriers were removed and the parties communicated, they could pool their knowledge, efforts, and resources to achieve the goal more quickly and efficiently. See Figure 2.2.

Although different perspectives and knowledge bases can be challenging as the team focuses on the common goal, these differences can broaden

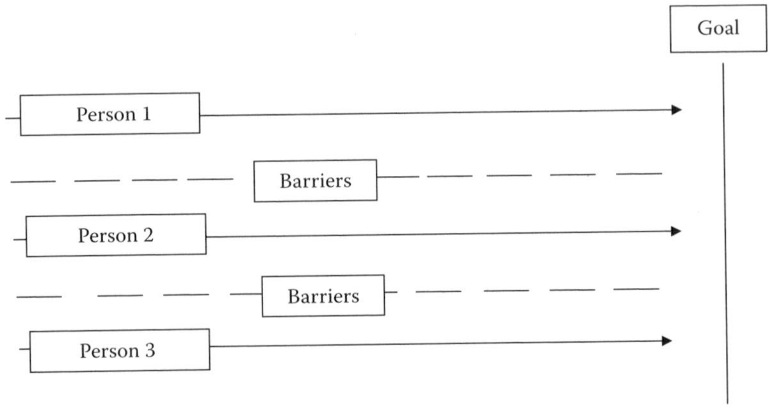

FIGURE 2.1
Parallel actions without communication. Each person is going down his or her own path heading in the same direction; however, the paths do not cross, and knowledge is not shared. If there are additional barriers to the communication such as people working on the same project but in different settings, they will not know what everyone's role is in the plan or if progress is being made. Each one may reach the common goal but may have used more resources and time because they did not merge their knowledge or resources.

the possibilities of how the goals are met. The plan is not restricted to one mindset but rather enhanced by the variety of the others' knowledge, experience, and approaches. Ground rules may need to be set for a clear understanding of expectations. Respect for each other while collaborating is important for effective communication.

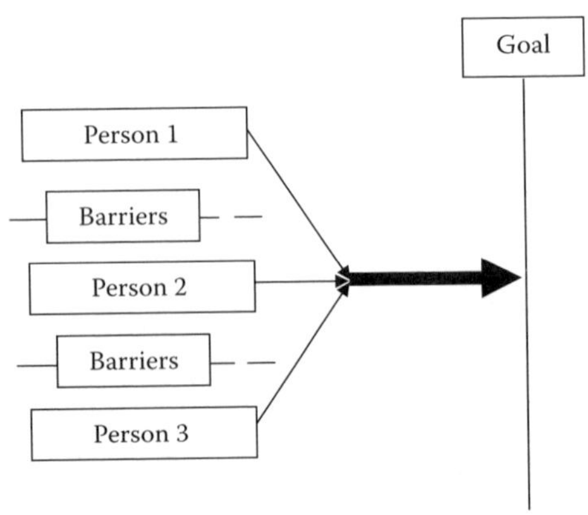

FIGURE 2.2
Parallel actions with communication. In comparison to Figure 2.1, Figure 2.2 demonstrates how if barriers are removed and each person merges his or her paths, the group can combine their efforts, knowledge, and experiences. As they communicate and collaborate, the goal is reached sooner, and potentially fewer resources may be used.

NURSING ROLES AND COLLABORATION

Nurses have various roles and responsibilities in healthcare, including direct nurse caregiver, charge nurse, or case manager. Collaboration within these nursing roles is vital for successful patient care. The nurse as the bedside caregiver may have different responsibilities and priorities than the charge nurse or nurse case manager; however, the overall picture should be the same. All should maximize their roles by using their knowledge and experience to enhance collaboration. Each entity has a wealth of information to share with his or her counterparts. Although these roles may vary in different organizations, the concept of working together is the important factor. The bedside nurse may be clinically savvy as he or she performs a thorough assessment of the patient's current condition applying his or her clinical knowledge. In addition, the bedside nurse has an understanding of the technical needs as he or she critically thinks through patient care. The charge nurse understands the staffing needs of the unit, admissions and discharges, physician orders, and ancillary department communication and provides leadership for a cohesive unit. The case manager's expertise includes understanding the dynamics of insurance or other payer's criteria, discharge needs of the patient, different levels of care, and various social aspects. An emerging role that correlates with these nursing positions is the clinical documentation specialist (CDS). Although the CDS is not a nurse in all organizations, the role will be viewed from a nursing perspective as described in Chapter 4. The CDS can integrate the information found on chart review with the clinical picture of the patient. Sharing this information with other disciplines provides a different but important aspect of the patient's overall status.

OTHER OPPORTUNITIES TO COLLABORATE

Opportunities to collaborate do not only occur within a specific role but are part of working together as a team. An example of collaboration is demonstrated when people work together to help each other. Collaboration does not always need to focus on the clinical aspects of care but may occur when someone needs help either asking for directions or finding a form.

For example, while working at the nurses' station, a staff member observes a visitor looking perplexed. The staff member asks if the visitor needs help. The visitor asks for directions to a specific unit, which the staff provides. Another staff member hears the request for directions and offers to take the person to the unit to avoid any confusion or further need for help. In another situation, a staff member appears to have technical difficulties with the computer system. Another staff member offers assistance and discovers it is not technical difficulties but a lack of understanding of how to use one of the computer programs. Not only does the staff member provide verbal assistance helping with the computer system, she also provides a resource for further assistance. Although both of these situations seem simple, they are examples of how basic collaboration can benefit others.

SUMMARY

Understanding communication styles and how people perceive different perspectives of knowledge can help a person with his or her own communication. Communication comes in many styles: *aggressiveness*, *passive-aggressiveness*, *passiveness*, and *assertiveness*. Understanding each type may help a person to communicate in the most effective style. Appropriate communication and behavior can affect patient safety. Using a template such as SBAR can facilitate communication in an organized manner. Besides understanding communication styles, one should understand different perspectives of knowledge, including personal, patient, or case perspectives. As one learns to work together and understand different roles, effective communication, trust, and collaboration may result. Successful communication creates a positive environment where people can work together for the benefit of the patient, team, and organization. In addition, successful communication is vital for safe, quality patient care.

REFERENCES

Iacono, M. 2003. Conflict, communication, and collaboration: Improving interactions between nurses and physicians. *Journal of PeriAnesthesia Nursing* 18:42–46.

Institute for Healthcare Improvement (IHI). n.d. SBAR technique for communication: A situational briefing model. http://www.ihi.org/IHI/Topics/PatientSafety/SafetyGeneral/Tools/SBARTechniqueforCommunicationASituationalBriefingModel.htm (accessed December 21, 2008).

The Joint Commission. 2008. Behaviors that undermine a culture of safety. Issue 40, July 9, 2008. http://www.jointcommission.org/SentinelEvents/SentinelEventAlert/sea_40.htm (accessed January 24, 2009).

The Joint Commission Accreditation. 2009. Hospital national patient safety goals. http://www.jointcommission.org/NR/rdonlyres/40A7233C-C4F7-4680-9861-80CDFD5F62C6/0/09_NPSG_HAP_gp.pdf (accessed November 9, 2009).

Lindeke, L., and A. Sieckert. 2008. Nurse-physician workplace collaboration. *Online Journal of Issues in Nursing.* http://www.nursingworld.org/mods/mod775/nrsderfull.htm (accessed November 19, 2008).

Microsoft Encarta Student 2006 DVD. *Microsoft® Encarta® 2006.* ©1993–2005 Microsoft Corporation.

Stein-Parbury, J., and J. Liaschenko. 2007. Understanding collaboration between nurses and physicians as knowledge at work. *American Journal of Critical Care* 16:470–77.

Zeiler, K. 2008. Assertive vs aggressive. *Advance for Nurses* 9:4.

3

Impacts: Quality and Financial

The focus of healthcare has gone beyond the clinical perspective of providing care. Although care should still be the first priority, quality and financial aspects influence how the care is delivered. One could argue that quality and financial characteristics should not drive healthcare; likewise, healthcare should not be considered a business. However, regardless of one's opinion, quality care and finance are part of the healthcare system. One could also debate that quality and finance are at two different ends of the spectrum. One may want quality care but does not understand the financial component. In contrast, one may have strong financial and business sense but not understand the importance of quality. How can both quality and financial responsibility be achieved at the same time? Fusing the two is vital for the success of an organization. Taking into consideration one's own health, would one not want care that consisted of safe, quality practices while considering the financial component?

As a consumer, we may consider quality and finance in our daily activities and not even realize it. Think about when we go to the grocery store to buy food. Do we buy the most expensive brand or the least expensive? Do we buy the best quality or the least? Although some may always want the best quality, it may cost more. We must weigh what we can afford with what we really want and need. This forces us to mesh and balance quality and finance together. Although we may want to purchase the best, unless there is a money tree growing in our backyard, most of us cannot afford to always have the best quality and the most expensive. Just as consumers assess the situation and balance their wants and needs, healthcare organizations must also figure how to provide the best quality care while considering the financial consequences of their decisions.

Keeping current on the quality and financial aspects can be a challenge. To add to the challenge, one must understand the verbiage related to terms that affect the financial and quality areas of healthcare. These terms are represented by many acronyms, which alone can be frustrating for someone attempting to muddle through the meanings of the "alphabet soup." Who thought when they went to college they would need to know what LOS, DRG, HAC, POA, and RAC mean? Were not acronyms and mnemonics used to learn anatomy, physiology, and disease processes? Now we must broaden our horizon to include these abbreviations in another light. How does a person accomplish this while keeping current with the clinical and technical aspects of his or her role? Knowing and understanding the meanings of various acronyms will help us understand the financial and quality aspects that correspond to the terms.

LENGTH OF STAY AND DIAGNOSIS-RELATED GROUPS

To begin with, one must learn what each acronym means. LOS is the acronym for *length of stay* as it pertains to how long a patient stays in the hospital. A patient's LOS may vary with different disease processes and overall health condition. Many years ago, patients would stay in the hospital for an undetermined period of time. In addition, patients would be admitted for testing that today would be done in an outpatient setting. However, in the 1980s, diagnosis-related groups (DRGs) were introduced. They indirectly affected how long the patient stayed in the hospital and the payment the hospital received. Medicare began reimbursing hospitals according to various diagnoses regardless of how long a patient stayed in the hospital. These diagnoses were attached to a DRG that also included an anticipated LOS. The LOS was a precalculated number of days for patients who are admitted with that DRG. However, the payment was not determined by the LOS but rather by the DRG. Because Medicare's payment was determined by the DRG and the principal reason the patient was admitted to the hospital, it was financially prudent for the hospital to manage its resources and the patient's LOS. For example, a 75-year-old woman is admitted with pneumonia and is generally weak because of her condition. However, the fact that she has pneumonia and weakness does not mean the patient should arbitrarily stay in the hospital until she is stronger. It may take 2 or 3 weeks before she is feeling "normal" again. If the patient is stable for discharge to another setting, such as the patient's home or a nursing home, the patient does not need to stay in the hospital to get stronger.

In addition to considering the LOS, hospitals also needed to consider what resources were needed to take care of the patient. Did the patient need the test or procedure for the patient's current condition, or was it a convenience to the patient to have the tests done while in the hospital for his or her illness? No longer would a patient be admitted for multiple tests that are not needed for the patient's current diagnosis or treatment plan during the stay when the tests can be done in an outpatient setting. For example, if the patient is admitted with pneumonia but is also due for her mammogram screening and colonoscopy, the mammogram and colonoscopy can be done later as an outpatient. The patient does not need to continue to stay in the hospital to have the outpatient procedures, as neither affect the patient's current treatment plan nor care of the patient's condition.

DRG

Even though Medicare pays many acute care facilities based on an inpatient prospective payment system (IPPS) using DRG assignments, other payers may also follow this payment concept. For this reason, it is important to be knowledgeable about how the DRG is determined. The DRG is determined by the patient's principal diagnosis. The Uniform Hospital Discharge Data Set (UHDDS) defines the principal diagnosis as "that condition established after study to be chiefly responsible for occasioning the admission of the patient to the hospital for care" (Advance, n.d.). Why was the patient admitted to the hospital? For example, a person may have the following diagnoses during his or her stay: pneumonia, cellulitis, and gastrointestinal bleeding. However, what was the main diagnosis that the patient came to and was admitted for at the hospital? Usually, this would be considered the principal diagnosis. The principal diagnosis is given a corresponding code number that is categorized into a DRG. DRGs are categorized under major diagnostic categories (MDCs). MDCs are generally organ-, system-, or condition-specific. These may include categories such as eye, circulatory, or respiratory systems or mental conditions, pregnancy, or infectious conditions. A DRG of pneumonia would be considered a respiratory system

MDC. As simple as this process sounds, complex coding rules such as sequencing of diagnosis and procedures affect this diagnosis. The intricate art of coding will not be addressed in this context; however, to simplify the basic process of matching a diagnosis to the DRG, see Figure 3.1.

Each DRG has a relative weight (RW) and an average LOS that has been predetermined by the previous use of resources for that DRG. Historically, how many resources have been used in the past for that DRG? What has been the average LOS for patients with this DRG? (For relevance to this

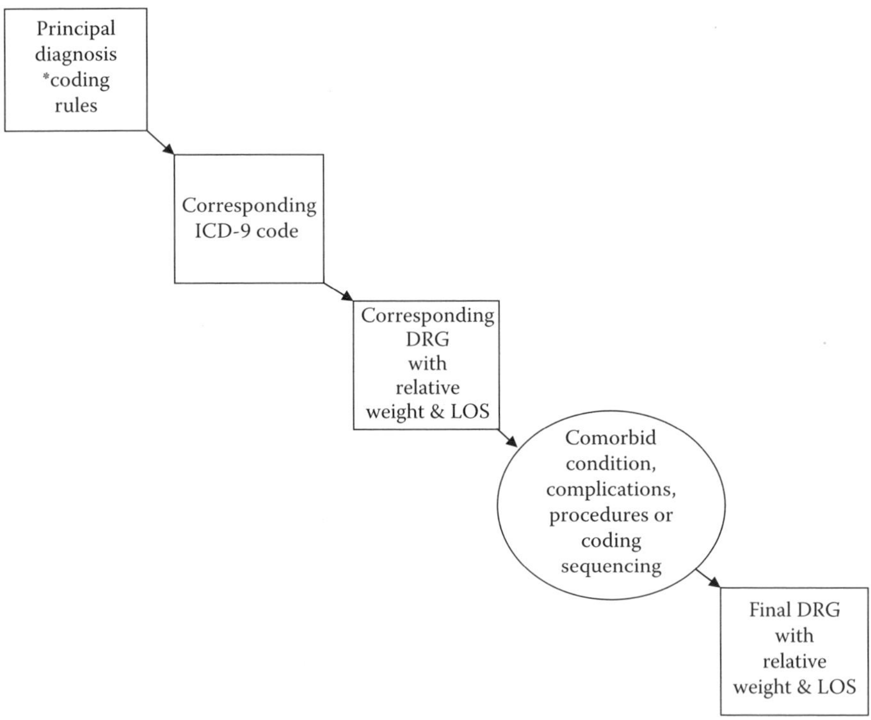

FIGURE 3.1
Diagnosis to DRG. The diagram demonstrates the thought process going from the principal diagnosis to the final DRG. While coding rules play an intricate role in determining the DRG, this diagram illustrates the basic process. Coding rules may include, but are not limited to, sequencing, procedures, and surgical impacts. One starts with the principal diagnosis that has a corresponding ICD-9 code. The ICD-9 codes are categorized under different DRGs. Each DRG has a corresponding predetermined relative weight and length of stay. Then additional diagnoses such as comorbid conditions, complications, procedures, and coding sequences are added to the process to determine the final DRG. This DRG may be different than what was initially determined from the principal diagnosis.

description, the LOS will be considered using the geometric mean LOS.) Each hospital is given a reimbursement rate that is multiplied by the DRG's RW to determine the Medicare reimbursement for that DRG. Generally, this is the amount the facility is paid by Medicare for the patient's hospital stay regardless of how extensive the stay is.

$$\text{Reimbursement rate} \times \text{DRG RW} = \text{Medicare reimbursement}$$

$$\$5{,}000 \times 1.5 = \$7{,}500$$

Previously, DRGs with RWs and LOS have been determined by considering a patient's age, complications, or comorbid conditions (CCs). The DRG system is updated annually starting with the October 1 discharges. Beginning with October 1, 2007 discharges, the DRG system added additional levels of payment depending on whether specific complications or comorbid conditions were considered major. Although these levels change annually, in 2009 a urinary tract infection (UTI) is considered a complication or comorbid condition, whereas pneumonia is considered a major complication or comorbid condition. The differences in the major or "not-major" conditions divide the DRG system into three potential tiers: a DRG without a complication or CC, a DRG with a CC, or a DRG with a major CC (MCC). Depending on the patient's principal diagnosis and his or her other health conditions, the patient would fall into one of these categories. See Figure 3.2.

As a general rule, the DRG with a CC would have a higher reimbursement and longer LOS than the same DRG without any additional CCs. In addition, the DRG with an MCC would have an even higher reimbursement and LOS than the same DRG with or without a CC. For example, consider the patient who is admitted with pneumonia versus the patient who is admitted with pneumonia and a Stage III pressure ulcer. Physicians caring for the patient with only pneumonia typically order a chest x-ray, blood cultures, complete blood count, and chemistry panel. The patient receives intravenous antibiotics, oxygen, and respiratory monitoring. The patient's lung sounds, oxygen saturation, temperature, and white blood cell count improve, and he or she can be discharged in 3 days. The patient's condition represents the basic DRG for pneumonia without a CC. In contrast, the patient admitted with pneumonia and a Stage III pressure ulcer on the coccyx requires the same treatment as the previous patient for pneumonia. However, because of the pressure

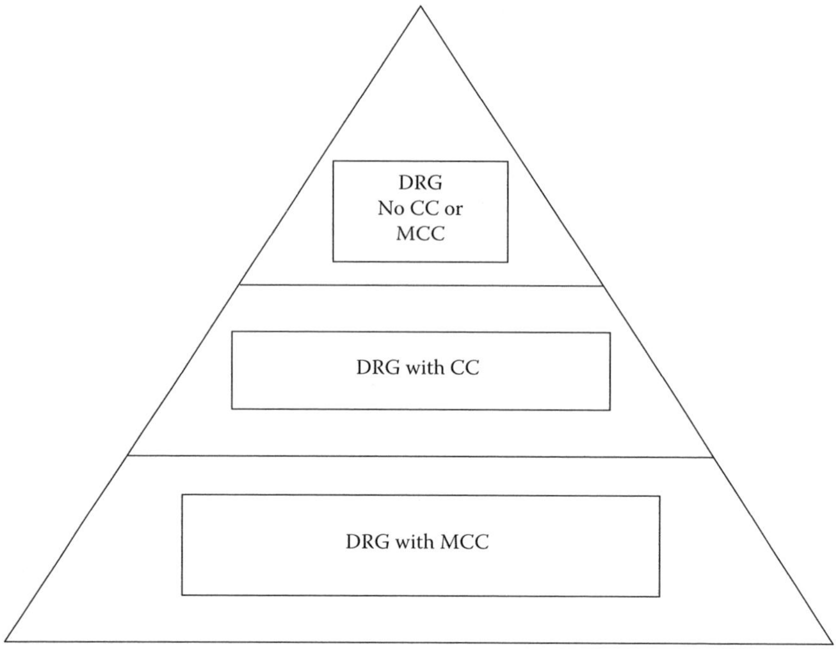

FIGURE 3.2
DRG pyramid. As the DRG changes from one without a CC or MCC to a DRG with a CC to a DRG with an MCC, the relative weight increases. The same DRG at the base of the triangle has a higher relative weight than the top of the triangle because a CC or MCC has been added. This increased relative weight reflects the potential need for the use of more resources with a complication or comorbid condition.

ulcer, the patient also requires a specialty mattress to reduce pressure, increased nursing care for positioning, and dressing care for the Stage III pressure ulcer. The patient's mattress has to be specially ordered, which is an additional cost. The pressure ulcer requires additional care and dressing changes because of the drainage. In addition, the patient had the pressure ulcer because of mobility problems. With decreased mobility, the patient does not clear secretions as well. The patient's respiratory status does not clear in 3 days and requires a change in the treatment plan. The DRG for this patient has an MCC, the Stage III pressure ulcer, included, which helps cover the resources needed for the additional care required for this patient. Thus, the different levels of the DRG system help reflect the increased LOS and resources needed to take care of the patient accordingly.

Unfortunately, not all additional diagnoses are considered CCs. Consider the patient who is admitted with pneumonia and has an abnormal cardiac rhythm of atrial fibrillation. In 2008–2009, atrial fibrillation was not considered a CC. This patient may be treated mainly for the pneumonia with little resources needed to manage the cardiac dysrhythmia. The heart rate and rhythm remain stable with the patient's oral cardiac medications. The pneumonia clears, and the patient can be discharged. In contrast, consider the same patient with pneumonia and atrial fibrillation who one evening complains of increased dyspnea. The nurse assesses the patient's lung sounds and obtains vital signs. The nurse notes the heart rate is elevated at 160 beats/min. The nurse calls the physician, who orders an electrocardiogram, which shows atrial fibrillation with a rapid ventricular response. The patient is transferred to the cardiac unit for continued telemetry monitoring and an intravenous antiarrhythmic medication. The patient's heart rate remains elevated and requires increased resources to control the rate. The patient continues to be treated for the pneumonia but now has an extended stay in the hospital until the heart rate and rhythm are controlled. Although this patient has an additional diagnosis of atrial fibrillation, it is not considered a CC. The atrial fibrillation does not change the DRG and the LOS; thus, reimbursement remains the same, as though the patient did not have any CCs. Although the DRG-based system has acknowledged some conditions that require increased resources to care for the patient properly, the system does not include all of the conditions that require extensive resources.

HOSPITAL-ACQUIRED CONDITIONS

Although there is potential for a higher reimbursement for the DRGs with a CC or MCC, a twist was added to the equation. This twist was part of the Deficit Reduction Act, in which hospitals are charged with managing their resources and taking accountability for various conditions. If the patient acquired a condition after admission to the hospital and the condition was on a list of specific diagnoses, the hospital would not get reimbursed at the higher rate for this condition. Thus, two more acronyms have become commonly used: POA (present on admission) and HAC (hospital-acquired condition). For example, if the patient had pneumonia but acquired a UTI related to the urinary catheter in the hospital, the DRG would normally have a CC, and the reimbursement would be higher than the DRG without a CC. However, because the catheter-associated UTI is on the HAC list, the UTI would not change the DRG, and reimbursement would remain as the basic pneumonia DRG.

The HACs were not randomly selected. According to the Centers for Medicare and Medicaid Services (CMS), these HACs were diagnoses that were considered high cost and/or volume, affecting a higher weighted DRG, and considered preventable. In addition, HAC does not affect all types of hospitals. According to CMS, some facilities that are exempt include long-term care hospitals, cancer treatment hospitals, and critical access hospitals to name a few (Centers for Medicare and Medicaid Services, Hospital-Acquired Conditions [Present on Admission Indicator]). It is vital for organizations to know whether they are affected by these HACs or are exempt.

The HAC list is not stagnant—indeed, it is frequently evaluated for changes. According to the CMS Fact Sheets, some of the HACs for 2008 included a condition in which a foreign object is retained after surgery, an air embolism, blood incompatibility, pressure ulcers (Stages III and IV), and specific falls and traumas, such as fractures and burns. In addition, some infectious-related HACs include catheter-associated UTIs, vascular catheter-associated infections, and certain surgical site infections. Although these may seem broad, there are specific International Statistical Classification of Diseases and Related Health Problems (ICD)-9 codes listed for these conditions. The list does not end here, as CMS continues to evaluate and update the HAC list with additional diagnoses. Staying current with these changes and participating in open forums are two ways to keep an organization on target.

Another concept that coincides with HAC is called "never events." Never events are part of the initiative from the National Quality Forums (NQF), because CMS noted that there are some conditions for which not only does it not want to pay but also should never occur, which are thus considered never events. The NQF calls never events serious reportable adverse events. According to the CMS Fact Sheet on Never Events, these are based on five criteria: "(1) unambiguous, (2) usually preventable, (3) serious, (4) indicative of a safety system problem, and (5) important for public accountability" (2008). However, there has been some confusion between serious reportable adverse events and HACs. Because they both have similar criteria, some people may think they are the same conditions. However, as mentioned previously, they have separate criteria. In addition, some conditions were on the HAC list but not on the serious reportable adverse events list. For example, in 2009, catheter-associated UTIs were on the HAC list but not on the serious reportable adverse events list. In contrast, a death or disability "associated with the use of contaminated drugs, devices, or biologics" was on the serious reportable adverse events list but not on the HAC list (CMS Fact Sheet, 2008). However, some conditions were on both lists, such as a foreign object left in a patient after surgery. This has caused some confusion, as some think that all HACs need to be reported. Again, this is another area that hospitals need to stay current with government regulations to understand the financial and quality impacts and changes.

PRESENT ON ADMISSION

Although not all conditions that occur after admission are on the HAC list, the POA status still needs to be addressed. Coding the accurate diagnoses is only part of completing the chart. The POA status must be addressed on coded conditions. CMS addresses general guidelines for reporting the POA. It must be determined whether the condition was (1) present at admission, (2) not present at admission, (3) unable to determine because of insufficient documented information, (4) unable to clinically determine by the provider, or (5) considered exempt from the reporting guideline. When the POA status of a condition is coded, the category into which it falls must be clear. In some cases, it is unclear whether the condition was POA, and the physicians will need to be asked. However, because the POA cannot be clearly defined for all diagnoses, even by the physician, the choice of unable to clinically determine is available. Although this is an option, it should not be used frequently when coding the POA status. In addition, just as with HAC, not all hospitals are affected by POA. According to CMS (Present on Admission Indicator Reporting, 2008), POA reporting pertains only to IPPS hospitals.

The POA status is determined by conditions that are present when the inpatient order for admission ensues. The key for POA is the inpatient order. Conditions that are acquired before inpatient admission are considered

POA. These include when the condition occurs in an outpatient clinic, outpatient surgery, emergency room, or during an observation stay. At times, it may be unclear whether the condition existed before admission and should be clarified by the physician or provider. The provider in this text "means a physician or any qualified health care practitioner who is legally accountable for establishing the patient's diagnosis" (CMS, Present on Admission Indicator Reporting, 2008, p. 2).

Documenting a thorough assessment of the patient on admission can support whether a condition was POA or a potential HAC. In addition, because HACs are considered preventable by the CMS, quality care is essential when taking care of patients. Incorporating evidence-based guidelines into patient care may help prevent these conditions.

IMPACTS OF DRGS, POA, AND HAC

So what does the impact of DRGs, POA, and HAC mean financially? According to the CMS, if a patient is admitted with the DRG 195 for simple pneumonia, the RW is 0.7316 (CMS, Table 5—List of MS-DRGs of the Federal Register, 2008). If the hospital has a reimbursement factor of $5,000 for a 1.0 RW, the payment would be $3,658 as calculated by 0.7316 × $5,000 = $3,658. However, if the patient is admitted with pneumonia and a UTI, the DRG would be 194, which includes a CC. This RW would be 1.0056 and would calculate to $5,028 (1.0056 × $5,000 = $5,028). However, if the patient has an MCC as defined by CMS, the DRG would be 193 with a RW of 1.4327 and the hospital's potential reimbursement of $7,163.50 (1.4327 × $5,000 = $7,163.50).

However, if the patient's UTI was not POA and is one of the diagnoses on the HAC list, then the UTI could not be considered a complication affecting the DRG. The DRG would remain 195 with the lower RW and reimbursement. The hospital would be paid $3,658 instead of $5,028, a difference of $1,370. If the patient had an MCC, which was not POA and was on the HAC list, the MCC could not be considered a major complication affecting the DRG. Instead of receiving a payment of $7,163.50, the facility would receive $3,658, a difference of $3,505.50. In addition, this patient required additional resources to take care of the HAC, which would cost the facility more. Regarding the LOS, the patient with pneumonia who had an MCC should have had a geometric mean LOS of 5.4 days. However, because the MCC was not POA and was on the HAC list, the LOS is calculated as 3.5 days. This shortens the projected LOS, even though potentially the patient's actual LOS is extended.

Although nurses and physicians can contribute to the quality of patient care, they can also affect the financial arena. These healthcare providers need to collaborate to provide quality care, but they also need to thoroughly document the patient's condition. By documenting a patient's signs and symptoms on admission and notifying the physician of any abnormal problems, conditions can be diagnosed and treated sooner. In addition, it may be easier to clarify whether the condition was POA by the documented signs and symptoms. For example, if the patient is admitted with pneumonia but also complains of lower abdominal discomfort, burning on urination, and has foul-smelling urine, the admitting nurse documents the symptoms and notifies the physician who orders a urinalysis and culture. When the urinalysis results are positive for a potential UTI, treatment can begin. In addition, because the signs and symptoms were documented on admission, the physician can determine more easily whether the UTI was POA and not a HAC.

POSTACUTE TRANSFER POLICY

The reimbursement for the value of the DRG's RW is not only affected by POA, HAC, MCC, and CC but also by the postacute transfer policy. According to the CMS, the postacute transfer policy is designed to decrease payment if the patient is transferred to a postacute setting, such as a skilled nursing facility (SNF) or home with home healthcare, before the DRG's geometric LOS. The postacute transfer policy does not apply to all DRGs but only specific ones. To explain further, one of the postacute transfer DRGs is 482. Consider a patient who is admitted with a fractured hip and has surgery. The potential DRG is 482 with a geometric mean LOS of 4.5 days. If the patient is discharged to an SNF at a 3-day LOS, the hospital will not get reimbursed for the entire DRG because the patient did not stay in the hospital the expected 4.5 days (Centers for Medicare and Medicaid Services, Descriptive Analysis of PAC Policy, 2008). Because of this postacute transfer policy, it is important that facilities have a plan to ensure the correct discharge status is entered on the bill when submitting it to Medicare. If the patient is discharged earlier than the postacute transfer DRG's predetermined LOS to an intermediate care nursing facility (ICF) and the discharge status is entered as an SNF, the discharge status will be incorrect. Then the acute care facility will receive a prorated DRG payment for the acute care stay because Medicare will think the patient went to a skilled facility. For example, if the DRG's payment was to be $2,000 and the patient left a day early, the payment may only be $1,500. The reverse could happen if the patient went to an SNF earlier than the predetermined DRG LOS and the discharge code was entered for an ICF. The facility would receive the full DRG payment when they should have received a prorated one. This incorrect status may be seen when the patient's SNF stay is billed and Medicare realizes the patient was discharged from a hospital before the DRG's expected LOS.

Ensuring the correct discharge status is entered correctly requires a collaborative process between nursing, coding, billing, and potentially case management. Did case management convey the correct discharge plan to nursing (i.e., SNF vs. ICF)? Was the discharge status entered correctly into the computer system? Was the correct DRG coded for the patient's stay? Did billing receive the correct DRG and discharge status? Was the patient discharged to the planned facility (i.e., ICF versus SNF or home with self-care vs. home with home healthcare)? These are some situations where collaboration affects accuracy, which can affect reimbursement.

The postacute transfer policy can become confusing as providers are encouraged to decrease the LOS on one hand but also are informed that keeping the patient in acute care is "ok" on the other hand. When the physician looks perplexed, further explanation may be needed regarding the postacute transfer policy and how it relates to a particular patient's condition. Although patients should not be kept in a hospital to fulfill a predetermined LOS, discharging them to another setting sooner than the expected LOS is reached may not be appropriate either. Every case should be evaluated to determine whether the patient is ready for discharge or should remain in the acute care setting for treatment. One patient may be ready for discharge to a lesser level of care, such as home with home healthcare or an SNF, whereas another may benefit from remaining in the hospital an additional day to continue treatment and monitor his or her condition. This additional day may be the determining factor of whether the discharge plan is successful or the patient is readmitted to the hospital in the near future.

Initially the postacute transfer list included 10 DRGs; however, it has now increased to 273 (CMS Fact Sheets, 2008). Whereas 10 DRGs may be easy to memorize, 273 is more than a little challenging. This provides another opportunity for nurses, physicians, case managers, and clinical documentation specialists (CDSs) to collaborate and apply the changes in regulations as the number of DRGs affected by the postacute transfer policy, HACs, and other factors continue to change. Although not everyone can know everything, knowing available resources is crucial when applying the information. Even bringing a heightened awareness to the disciplines can help the process, as all workers begin to realize the quality and financial components affecting healthcare.

OUTLIER PAYMENTS

While the DRG payment is affected by CCs, MCCs, HAC, POA, and the postacute transfer policy, Medicare reimbursement is also affected by another factor. Because organizations take care of people with their own idiosyncrasies, one cannot always predict outcomes. There are circumstances when irrespective of how an organization tries to provide efficient, quality care, the patient's condition fluctuates and incurs high costs. These costs are more than a little over the expected reimbursement but on the extreme end of the spectrum. The CMS recognizes some patients' hospital stays may acquire such astronomical costs and has created outlier payments for Medicare-participating hospitals. The outlier concept depends on a cost-to-charge ratio. The complex calculation for the outlier payment includes various factors, such as the DRG RW, operating costs, and capital costs. The CMS website has provided an outlier example spreadsheet called the Outlier Example FY2007 to assist with understanding the calculation. This spreadsheet can be found at http://www.cms.hhs.gov/acuteinpatientpps/04_outlier.asp and is available as a download on the CMS website. According to CMS, "a case must have costs above a fixed-loss cost threshold amount (a dollar amount by which the costs of a case must exceed payments in order to qualify for outliers)."

A patient qualifying for an outlier payment may be someone who has required an extraordinary long LOS, care, and costs such as multiple surgeries and complications. This may be a patient who only stabilizes briefly and then requires intense costly interventions or procedures. The patient's underlying condition may be such that despite how well his or her case is managed, the patient's condition fluctuates, warranting expanded services, procedures, and care. According to the DRG, the expected reimbursement might be $18,000; however, the patient has incurred a bill of $280,000. This type of patient billing should be reviewed for a potential outlier payment.

PUBLIC REPORTING

LOS, DRG, HACs, and POA are not the only areas that affect healthcare. Another aspect is public reporting of clinical indicators. The public is becoming more consumer-aware because it has access to various types of healthcare information via the Internet. Some of this information, such as clinical indicators, focuses on the quality of hospitals. However, the information must first be gathered and submitted for it to be made public. Hospitals have staff review patients' charts collecting specific data according to abstraction guidelines. The review consists of specific quality indicators to assess the care given to patients according to specific measures. For example, if reviewing a chart for a patient with pneumonia, some of the quality indicators may include that blood cultures were drawn before the administration of antibiotics and the time the initial antibiotic was given. If the documentation to support the quality indicators is not in the chart or if the indicator does not meet the designated time, the chart does not meet the quality indicators. After the chart abstraction, the information is submitted, and the data are analyzed. Initially this was a volunteer reporting program focusing on quality aspects of myocardial infarction, pneumonia, and heart failure. These indicators were not haphazardly chosen but were constructed from precise evidence, supporting guidelines, and care standards.

One may ask why an institution should be subjected to reporting these data if it is not required, because such review takes time and resources. However, there was a financial incentive for the organization to participate in the reporting. The quality measures have grown from the original 10 to a projected 42 for 2010. Some of these include 30-day readmissions for heart failure, postoperative dehiscence of a wound, iatrogenic pneumothorax, and mortality for certain medical conditions or surgical conditions (CMS Fact Sheets, 2008).

Although collecting data is important, it is the outcome that can make the difference. Thus came the next phase: Medicare's hospital value-based purchasing program (VBP). This program focuses on the performance of the hospital and not just the ability to report data. This program puts even more pressure on organizations to be proactive with quality care because payments would be adjusted by performance. The payments to the hospital would be affected by their performance (U.S. Department of Health and Human Services, n.d.).

The consumer can see how a hospital performs according to predetermined measures for specific conditions. Through a website such as Hospital Compare the public can compare hospitals from three different aspects (http://www.hospitalcompare.hhs.gov, n.d.). One is the patient's experience during his or her stay; another is the percentage that the care is given according to recommended treatment; and the third is the outcome or results of a patient's care. Some of the diagnoses and surgical procedures that are measured include heart failure, chest pain, chronic lung disease, back and neck operations, heart bypass surgery, and intestinal operations. People can compare the data among three different hospitals, the average of hospitals within the state, and the average of hospitals in the United States that report their data. Although this does not represent every quality aspect of a hospital, it gives the consumer a snapshot of how different facilities rate among each other.

Hospital Compare is not the only website available for consumers. HealthGrades is another site that provides an array of information about various providers (http://www.healthgrades.com). For hospitals, some of the comparison focuses on the complications or mortality of certain health conditions or surgeries. Although HealthGrades and Hospital Compare are two different entities, they both provide information to help the public be more knowledgeable consumers.

Accuracy of data collection and documentation is crucial because this information is captured and displayed to the public. If the information is not collected appropriately or the documentation does not support the true diagnosis of the patient, inaccurate information will be presented. An example would be if the patient is admitted with the diagnosis of pneumonia but really has acute bronchitis. The data collected will be applied as though the patient had pneumonia. However, because the patient did not have pneumonia and was treated for acute bronchitis, the information should not have been applied to the pneumonia data collection. Another example would be if the principal diagnosis is listed as a UTI. However, the patient really had sepsis, but it was not documented. The patient is critically ill and dies. According to the principal diagnosis, it looks as though the patient died having a UTI instead of the correct diagnosis of sepsis. This does not represent the true clinical picture of the patient, and these skewed data misrepresent the true picture for the organization and the quality care it provides.

Physicians, nurses, case managers, and CDSs have the opportunity to help with these quality indicators by addressing them concurrently while the patient is in the hospital. Although it may sound obvious to provide quality care, incorporating these quality indicators into the daily process may seem like one more thing to do. However, if the team of healthcare workers collaborates and incorporates the quality indicators into the daily process, the potential to meet these expectations improves. These healthcare workers should be educated on the indicators and their role in the process. The indicators can be incorporated into preprinted orders. In addition, a checklist can be created with the indicators and placed on each patient's chart. As case managers and CDSs review the patient's chart, they can compare the patient's care and information to the quality indicator checklist. If the patient meets criteria for the indicators and they have not been addressed, the case manager and/or CDS can speak with the nurse and physician regarding the part that needs to be addressed. If it is an educational component such as congestive heart failure or smoking cessation education, the nurse can provide the education. However, if the patient needs a test or medication ordered according to the quality indicators, the physician will need to be contacted. This does not mean the physician will always need to order the test or medication; however, he or she should document in the chart why the test or medication was not ordered. If this collaborative effort occurs while the patient is in the hospital, the quality indicators can be met. Although chart abstraction still needs to occur after the patient is discharged and the chart is coded, the potential to have better outcomes is greater if done earlier.

RECOVERY AUDIT CONTRACTORS

The government is not only looking at the aforementioned quality and financial aspects of healthcare but also the accuracy and appropriateness of service. Through the Medicare Prescription Drug, Improvement, and Modernization Act of 2003, the Department of Health and Human Services was charged with managing a program to identify and rectify improper payments made on Medicare Fee-for-Service claims (Centers for Medicare and Medicaid Services, n.d.). The program was referred to as the Recovery Audit Contractors (RACs). This 3-year demonstration project was initially rolled out in California, Florida, and New York. The RAC reviewed claims for improper payments. There were two types of reviews: automated and complex. The automated reviews did not require a chart review, whereas the complex ones did. For the complex review, organizations would have to provide the RACs with the patient's medical record information to determine whether an improper payment was made.

Inpatient hospitals were not the only areas targeted. In addition, some of the others under scrutiny included inpatient rehabilitation facilities, SNFs, physician services, and durable medical equipment providers. Many improper payments were directed toward lack of medical necessity and incorrect coding. These included surgical procedures or medical treatments not being done in the appropriate setting or not having the accurate documentation to support the coded condition or procedure. An example would be if a patient had a wound debridement and the chart was coded as excisional debridement, but the documentation in the chart only included the verbiage of sharp debridement. The lack of specific wording did not support excisional debridement. Another example of medical necessity would be if a patient was admitted as an inpatient for a procedure that could have been done safely in an outpatient setting.

Other issues that may occur are when patients are discharged with home healthcare or to an SNF, but the discharge code was entered as "home with self-care." If the DRG is included as part of the postacute transfer policy and the patient was discharged before the geometric mean LOS, the organization should have received a prorated DRG payment instead of the full amount. Another concern is if two identical procedures were billed for the same patient on the same day. Was this duplicate billing, or was it incorrectly coded? Other areas are patients who were admitted as inpatients but discharged with a 1-day LOS. Did these patients really meet inpatient criteria? These issues were targets for incorrect payments. Although the RAC was looking for improper payments, most were found to be overpayments, 96% or $992.7 million dollars, compared with underpayments, 4% or $37.8 million dollars (Centers for Medicare and Medicaid Services, 2008). Organizations will have the ability to appeal the RAC's decision, but this will take time and resources. Although the RAC was paid on contingency, the money they recouped back to the Medicare Trust Fund outweighed the cost of the program. Because of the success of the program, the Tax Relief and Health Care Act of 2006 required a permanent RAC program across the United States by 2010.

Considerations for Preparing for RAC

This RAC mandate encourages organizations to examine their own practices. Organizations should create a multidisciplinary team to prepare for RAC. Team members should include those who understand clinical, coding, case management, utilization review, appeals process, compliance, billing, and revenue cycles. The team should prepare by performing internal audits. These audits may range from evaluation for appropriateness of patient status to 1-day inpatient stays to accuracy in coding. Although the organization may not think it has many concerns in these areas, an internal audit may show differently. When the concerns of medical necessity, 1-day stays, and coding discrepancies are tallied and calculated into a dollar figure, the amount may be astonishing. In addition, because this money will need to be paid back to the Medicare Trust Fund, organizations will have to consider how they can manage this financial loss.

Ensuring a patient is admitted with the correct status, inpatient versus observation, according to established criteria is one area to audit. Organizations might use established written criteria to facilitate determination of the patient's status. However, one should remember this criterion may not be completely absolute and should consider the patient holistically. When considering whether a patient's admission and continued stay meet criteria, one must assess the patient's condition and treatment plan. When assessing whether the patient's condition meets inpatient status, examine the patient's objective, measurable clinical findings. These may be specific diagnostic values such as lab results or presenting symptoms such as vomiting. The patient's severity of condition is not equivalent to the diagnosis alone. Just because a patient has a diagnosis of congestive heart failure, he or she needs to have supporting clinical symptoms and/or diagnostics to support the severity of the condition. The treatment plan is the type and frequency of treatments or monitoring required for the care of the patient in the particular setting.

Once the clinical picture is examined and applied to admission criteria, the patient should be admitted with the appropriate status. According to the CMS Medicare Benefit Policy Manual, observation is considered a period when one can provide short-term specific clinical interventions, monitoring, and reassessments of a patient's condition to determine whether the patient needs to be admitted as an inpatient status or can be discharged. This decision can usually be made within less than 48 hours, if not even by 24 hours. From here the patient's condition and treatment should be examined to see whether the patient's treatment is still intense enough to require an inpatient setting. Just because a patient's condition and intense treatment met criteria to be admitted initially does not mean he or she continues to meet criteria for the rest of the hospital stay. Thus, discharge planning should be initiated on admission.

Once the patient is discharged, the chart is sent for coding. Here the coder has the responsibility to review the documentation and apply the codes according to coding guidelines. Because of the complexity of coding, one should be astute in his or her ability and knowledge to code appropriately. Understanding the impact of the accuracy of appropriate status, documentation, and coding and applying the information are crucial for successful compliance with CMS and other governing bodies.

Preparing for RACs is vital for an organization. Besides building a team to prepare for RAC, a liaison should be chosen as the RAC contact person. This person is charged with keeping current with RAC updates and activity. Because the liaison should be the most knowledgeable with current RAC information, he or she should disseminate the information to others in the organization. The RAC contact person should coordinate educational sessions for physicians, nurses, administration, coders, case managers, CDSs, and compliance, billing, and financial staff on RAC updates. In addition, this person should oversee the organization's multidisciplinary team developing a plan to respond to RAC requests, denials, and potential appeals. Developing a spreadsheet with specific time frames to track chart requests, note responses, and write appeals is crucial in avoiding denials resulting from lack of timely responses. When a copy of the chart is requested and sent for review, the information should be logged with the potential response date. This information should be followed so that if a denial does occur, the appeal can be written in the designated time frame. The appeal should also be logged with an expected response date to prevent the appeal from being lost in the system. The appeals process can become very complex and time consuming. Having an organized proactive approach with a knowledgeable leader and multidisciplinary team can facilitate this process.

SUMMARY

Healthcare is targeted from many angles to comply with quality and financially sound practices. Understanding the linkage between the patient's principal diagnosis, DRGs, LOS, RWs, and reimbursement is important from a financial perspective. However, financial impacts do not end here, as HACs and POA affect the assigned DRG. The medical record's information does not just affect finances but also quality because data are collected from chart review. This information is submitted and placed on websites, such as Hospital Compare, so the public can evaluate how organizations rate against each other. Public reporting is just the beginning of assessing quality, as the next step, VBP, considers actual outcomes. Then, just when an organization is learning how to manage these financial and quality issues, the RACs enter into the equation—performing retro reviews for coding and medical necessity. Keeping current with these changes challenges organizations. Considering the complexity of the financial and quality aspects of healthcare and the future of RAC, it is prudent for various disciplines within an organization to collaborate for the success of the organization and patient care.

REFERENCES

Advance for Health Information Professionals. n.d. Principal diagnosis conundrums: How to interpret "evolving" diagnosis. http://health-information.advanceweb.com/editorial/content/editorial.aspx?cc=74412 (accessed February 8, 2009).

Advance for Health Information Professionals. http://health-information.advanceweb.com/Editorial/Content/Editorial.aspx?CC=74412 (accessed February 8, 2009).

Centers for Medicare and Medicaid Services. n.d. Descriptive analysis of PAC policy change. http://www.cms.hhs.gov/AcuteInpatientPPS/downloads/chap2.pdf (accessed February 8, 2009).

Centers for Medicare and Medicaid Services. n.d. Fact sheets. Details for CMS proposes additions to list of hospital-acquired conditions for fiscal year 2009. http://www.cms.hhs.gov/apps/media/press/factsheet.asp?Counter=3042&intNumPerPage=10&checkDate=&checkKey=&srchType=1&numDays=3500&srchOpt=0&srchData=&keywordType=All&chkNewsType=6&intPage=&showAll=&pYear=&year=&desc=false&cboOrder=date (accessed December 28, 2008).

Centers for Medicare and Medicaid Services. n.d. Hospital-acquired conditions (present on admission indicator). http://www.cms.gov/HospitalAcqCond (accessed January 8, 2009).

Centers for Medicare and Medicaid Services. n.d. *Medicare Benefit Policy Manual.* Hospitals covered under part B. Chapter 6. http://www.cms.hhs.gov/manuals/Downloads/bp102c06.pdf (accessed February 17, 2009).

Centers for Medicare and Medicaid Services. n.d. RAC demonstration. http://www.cms.hhs.gov/RAC/02_ExpansionStrategy.asp (accessed February 6, 2009).

Centers for Medicare and Medicaid Services. 2007. Outlier payments. http://www.cms.hhs.gov/AcuteInpatientPPS/04_outlier.asp (accessed March 28, 2009).

Centers for Medicare and Medicaid Services. 2008. Fact sheets. Details for CMS improves patient safety for Medicare and Medicaid by addressing never events. http://www.cms.hhs.gov/apps/media/press/factsheet.asp (accessed June 6, 2009).

Centers for Medicare and Medicaid Services. 2008. Fact sheets. Details for fiscal year 2009 quality measure reporting for 2010 payment update. http://www.cms.hhs.gov/apps/media/press/factsheet.asp?Counter=3225&intNumPerPage=10&checkDate=&checkKey=&srchType=1&numDays=3500&srchOpt=0&srchData=&keywordType=All&chkNewsType=6&intPage=&showAll=&pYear=&year=&desc=false&cboOrder=date (accessed February 17, 2009).

Centers for Medicare and Medicaid Services. 2008. Fact sheets. Details for proposed fiscal year 2009 payment, policy changes for inpatient stays in general acute care hospitals. http://www.cms.hhs.gov/apps/media/press/factsheet.asp?Counter=3045&intNumPerPage=10&checkDate=&checkKey=&srchType=1&numDays=3500&srchOpt=0&srchData=&keywordType=All&chkNewsType=6&intPage=&showAll=&pYear=&year=&desc=false&cboOrder=date (accessed February 8, 2009).

Centers for Medicare and Medicaid Services. 2008. The Medicare recovery audit contractor (RAC) program: An evaluation of the 3-year demonstration. June 2008. http://www.cms.hhs.gov/RAC/Downloads/RAC%20Evaluation%20Report.pdf (accessed February 6, 2009).

Centers for Medicare and Medicaid Services. 2008. Table 5—List of MS-DRGs, relative weighting factors, and geometric & arithmetic mean length of stay. FY 2009 final rule. *Federal Register* 73:161.

HealthGrades. n.d. http://www.healthgrades.com (accessed February 7, 2009).

Present on Admission (POA) Indicator Reporting by Acute Inpatient Prospective Payment System (IPPS) Hospitals. 2008. http://www.cms.hhs.gov/HospitalAcqCond/Downloads/POAFactsheet.pdf (accessed January 8, 2009).

U.S. Department of Health and Human Services. n.d. Hospital Compare: A quality tool provided by Medicare. http://www.hospitalcompare.hhs.gov (accessed February 7, 2009).

U.S. Department of Health and Human Services. n.d. HHS action plan to prevent health-care-associated infections: Incentives and oversight. http://hhs.gov/ophs/initiatives/hai/incentives.html (accessed January 21, 2009).

4

Clinical Documentation Specialist: Who Is Involved and What Is the Process?

Documentation is one of the tools used in healthcare to communicate information. This information is not only used by physicians, nurses, and other healthcare providers but also by people working in other disciplines and departments within an organization. The physical therapist, dietician, and social worker may be some obvious hands who touch the chart; however, the list also includes the case manager, hospital coders, the billing office, and possibly risk management workers. From the information obtained in the clinical record, information is sent to payers, government agencies, or other financial or quality organizations. Therefore, the documentation should represent an accurate clinical picture of the patient and vice versa. Although many resources may be available regarding the "dos and don'ts" of nursing documentation, this reference will focus on the accuracy of physician documentation. The clinical documentation specialist (CDS) role intertwines clinical knowledge and coding attributes to assess for accurate documentation of the patient's condition by the physician in the medical record.

The CDS role may fall under different departments within an organization. Some may place the role under health information management (HIM), quality, or case management. The reporting structure will depend on the organization. What is important is the role the CDS performs. The CDS does not function within a bubble of his or her own world; rather, the role intertwines with other departments. As mentioned in Chapter 2, people need to communicate to collaborate. All entities need to understand how they affect others, either directly or indirectly. This domino effect can be seen if one looks at the big picture and not only at one's own role.

Consider the initial admission process for a patient and all the disciplines involved. If the patient is admitted through the physician's office, the physician or his or her designee will need to contact the hospital for the admission. This point of contact may be the nursing supervisor or an admission bed center. Information is gathered about the patient's condition and needs. Next, a bed assignment is made, and the receiving nursing unit is notified of the admission. The patient's information is entered into the computer system, so when the patient arrives the information will only need to be confirmed. The patient may need to supply identification and payer information to confirm that the data in the computer system are accurate. From here, treatment consent forms are signed, and the patient is transported to the nursing unit. Although this sounds like a basic process, many steps and communication occur, including the physician's office to the nursing supervisor to the admission staff and a verbal or written confirmation with the patient. This process does not include behind-the-scenes information that is generated from the computer system and communicated with the case management staff, billing office, CDS, and other departments in the organization. If each entity attempted to admit the patient into the hospital without the collaboration of other departments, the process could be long and confusing, and an overlap of resources and processes could result. Good communication within an organization provides for fluent patient care and processes.

CDS ROLE

The CDS may be given different titles depending on the individual organization. One organization may use the title of clinical documentation management professional (CDMP), whereas others may use CDS. It is not the specific name that matters but the role it fulfills in the organization. The role focuses on accuracy of physician documentation based on the patient's condition and clinical record. The CDS may have different experience backgrounds; the two primary ones are registered nurse (RN) or HIM coding professional. Although workers from the two specialties may perform the CDS role, in this context the CDS role will be considered from a nurse's perspective. In addition, although understanding that coding is an integral part of the CDS role, coding is not the focus of this book. Instead, the RN will use his or her clinical expertise to integrate documentation with the coding world. A joint effort between the two entities is vital for the success of the program.

CDS PROCESS

Although organizations may structure the CDS role differently, this reference will describe a process that has been successful for this author. The basic process consists of concurrent chart reviews by the CDS while simultaneously communicating with the coders. The CDS performs a complex chart review while the patient is in the hospital. The CDS also reviews the physician's documentation as it relates to the patient's clinical signs, symptoms, diagnostics, and treatment plan. From this information, the CDS determines the potential principal diagnosis and categorizes the patient under a working diagnosis-related group (DRG) (as explained in Chapter 3). Because the information is reviewed concurrently, the working DRG may change throughout the patient's stay depending on the patient's condition and physician documentation. As the CDS finds areas that need further documentation or clarification, the CDS asks the physician for more information. The CDS may do this on a written query form or verbally. However, addressing documentation in a real time approach instead of retrospectively provides many opportunities to communicate issues while the chart is still active.

Today's computer technology provides many avenues to develop a CDS program. Creating a daily work list is important to capture new admissions and concurrent reviews. The work list may be handwritten or computer-generated. Depending on the needs of the organization, the work list may contain the patient's name, room number, attending physician, the current DRG, the DRG's geometric mean length of stay (LOS), and the patient's actual LOS. This allows the CDS to review actual versus projected information. For example, one can see when the patient's actual LOS has gone over the projected LOS for the DRG. This information can be communicated with the case management staff to help guide them on the projected LOS versus the actual LOS for discharge planning.

This link between the CDS and case manager provides an opportunity for collaboration.

CDS Worksheet

From the work list, a worksheet should be generated for each patient. The worksheet can be created from a template in a computer program. The CDS may handwrite on this worksheet or document on the worksheet in a computerized program provided by a vendor. There are many vendors available, and each organization will have to evaluate its need for a specialized or formal program through a vendor versus creating its own system. However, the concept of the worksheet should consist of demographic information such as the patient's name, admission date, medical record number, account number, birth date, and room number. These demographic areas may be automatically populated if using a computerized system. The worksheet should also contain headings for the primary diagnosis, secondary diagnoses, procedures, diagnostic results, and medical history. Although some of the clinical information such as the diagnosis may be automatically entered, the CDS must remember there needs to be supporting physician documentation for the diagnosis—not only what was entered by a computer program. For example, if the admitting nurse enters pneumonia for the reason for admission in the computer system, this is not a documented diagnosis by the physician. The physician has to document the patient's diagnosis. Therefore, the CDS reviews the chart for the physician's documentation of the diagnoses, procedures, and medical history. Procedures should be listed to monitor whether any would potentially change the DRG, such as a surgical procedure overriding a medical principal diagnosis. Other headings on the worksheet provide a reminder of locations to find information, such as nursing, therapy, and social worker's documentation. In addition, the CDS should review the patient's vital signs, height, weight, pulse oximetry, and other clinical data. Diagnostics such as lab and x-ray results should be reviewed for abnormal findings. All of these provide potential clues of other conditions the patient may have but perhaps are not captured in the original documented diagnosis. Because physician documentation is required when coding the chart, it is important for the CDS to keep track of what information the physician has documented versus potential areas of documentation from supporting data. The CDS should look in the history and physical examination notes, consult notes, and progress notes for the physician's documentation.

The CDS completes each section of the worksheet to keep the information organized. Each time the CDS reviews the chart, he or she can write the date of the review and corresponding information. In addition, the worksheet should include an area for queries that need follow-up as a reminder to the CDS as to what has been asked. See Figure 4.1.

Working DRG	**Admit date**	**Medical record number**	**Account number**	**Name** **Birth date** **Room number**
Admit diagnosis		**Procedures**		
Nurse, therapy, dietician, social worker, etc. assessment/ documentation	**Vitals, pulse ox, clinical data**	**Diagnostics**	**Treatments**	**Physician's documentation/ diagnosis (history and physical, consult notes, progress notes, etc.)**
Review date				
Review date				
Review date				
Potential queries			**Follow-up**	

FIGURE 4.1
Sample CDS worksheet.

Unit-Based versus Physician-Based Model

Another step in developing the CDS process is to determine how the patients will be divided among the CDSs. What is an appropriate ratio of patients per CDS? Will each CDS take an average of 30 patients to review? How will new patients be distributed among the CDSs? This may depend on whether the CDS has other functions besides the CDS role or the type of model that will be used in the organization.

Two main approaches are the unit-based and the physician-based models (see Figure 4.2). With the unit-based model, the CDS might review patients only on certain units. One CDS may specialize in reviewing the telemetry and critical care units, whereas another CDS reviews the medical, surgical, and orthopedic units. With the physician-based approach, a CDS reviews a patient's chart information depending on the attending physician or physician call group. The CDS may examine all patients' charts for physician call group A, and another CDS examines the charts for physician call group B. Both approaches have pros and cons.

The unit-based approach allows the CDS to concentrate on each unit's specialty and disease processes and the documentation that corresponds with this population. In addition, the CDS and unit nurses may build a rapport as they work together on each unit. The disadvantage of this

	Unit-based	**Physician-based**
Description	CDS assigned to specific units.	CDS assigned to specific physicians or physician groups.
Pros	Able to concentrate on disease processes or populations of a specific unit. CDS and unit nurses build rapport as they work together.	CDS builds rapport with assigned physicians or physician call group. Learns what works best for communication with each physician. When the patient transfers from unit to unit, the CDS follows the patient, which allows continuity.
Cons	When the patient transfers to another unit, the CDS does not follow. Loses continuity as the receiving CDS does not know the history of the patient or previous documentation.	May need to know a variety of disease processes.

FIGURE 4.2
Unit-based versus physician-based model.

method is when a patient transfers from one unit to another the CDS does not follow the patient and chart documentation. Another CDS on the receiving unit will follow this patient's chart documentation. This creates a disconnect, as another CDS has to know where one set of information and documentation stopped and another begins.

In contrast, a physician-based model allows the CDS to build rapport with the physicians in the call group. This alliance may promote building trust, teamwork, and communication. Moreover, as the team works together there are opportunities to share knowledge and education. In addition, when the patient transfers to another unit, the CDS follows the patient from unit to unit. This provides a fluent, consistent approach with review and follow-up work. Regardless of how the organization chooses to run the CDS program, there should be consistency in the approach. In addition, the CDS must maintain credibility with healthcare providers through trust, respect, accuracy, and follow-through with communication.

Chart Review

After the patients are divided among the CDSs according to their work lists, the worksheets should be printed and organized for each CDS to review. If a computer or a vendor with a specific system is used, the work list may be maintained on the computer. If a paper system is used, the sheets may be organized in a notebook. Again, the preference of using a manual versus an automated program will need to be evaluated by each organization. Although manual systems may run the risk of human error by manually transposing numbers or data, an automated system may be costly. In addition, automated computer systems might need to be compatible with other computer systems the organization is using and can require upgrades or maintenance.

After the worksheet is printed and the patient assignments are divided among the CDS staff, the CDS can begin the chart review by examining the clinical record. The CDS should review the physician's progress notes, lab results, x-rays, therapy notes, dietary notes, nurse's notes, and other disciplines. When performing a chart review, a systematic approach helps with consistency, organization, and accuracy. One approach is to begin with the history and physical examination, which should include an impression of the patient's condition on admission. This should give a good basis for a working diagnosis or diagnoses. Next, proceed to consult notes, physician orders, and progress notes. If the patient is admitted through the emergency room, this part of the chart can provide information about the initial severity of his or her condition. Then, review the nurse's admission assessment, which gives another perspective of what the patient reports as a history and the initial assessment. The nurse's assessment may use a specific template, which covers areas such as vital signs, height, weight, pulse oximetry, home medications, review of systems, home assessment needs, and past surgical and medical conditions. After reviewing the admission assessment, review any shift assessments, nurse's notes, diagnostic reports, procedure notes, and dietary, social work, physical therapy, and other discipline notes. Using the worksheet to track pertinent data keeps the information organized. See Figure 4.3 for how each area is completed from the information obtained upon chart review. At the bottom of the worksheet is a place to write potential queries that need follow-up. Remember this is not the query form but only a worksheet the CDS uses to keep information organized. In some cases, the information in the potential query area may be what the CDS is considering writing concerning a query, but he or she is waiting for further information before actually writing on the query form.

After gathering the information, the CDS should determine the principal diagnosis as defined by the Uniform Hospital Discharge Data Set noted in Chapter 3. The CDS next assesses for additional diagnoses. According to Coding Clinic (2005), these diagnoses would affect the care of the patient by necessitating clinical evaluation, diagnostic procedures, an increase in the LOS in the hospital, therapeutic care interventions or treatment, or an increase in nursing care or monitoring. A previous diagnosis that has no bearing on these areas should not be coded or queried for the physician to document. An example may be if the patient has had a history of pneumonia but is no longer receiving treatment or exhibiting symptoms. This diagnosis would not be considered an additional diagnosis. After considering the above criteria and reviewing the chart, the CDS documents on a query form questions or clarifications for the physician to address.

Query Aspects

When the CDS must ask a physician about his or her documentation, the CDS should write the question on a form. This query form is used for communication with the physician regarding queries and documentation. The form can be used to document the written query but can also be used to

Working DRG 195	**Admit date** 9/23/09	**Medical record number** M2340212	**Account number** A19283777	**Name** Sandra Smith **Birth date** 03/12/32 **Room number** 415A
Admit diagnosis Pneumonia		**Procedures** 9/24 Bronchoscopy		
Nurse, therapy, dietician, social worker, etc. assessment/ documentation	**Vitals, pulse ox, clinical data**	**Diagnostics**	**Treatments**	**Physician's documentation/ diagnosis (history and physical, consult notes, progress notes, etc.)**
Review date 9/24 Dyspnea, lung sounds: wheezes throughout, productive cough, green sputum From nursing home	T102.4 92% 4L O2 100-26	CXR-infiltrate on Rt WBC 20.2 Bands 19 Bronch cx: Pending___ Blood cx: Pending___ Na 121 Repeat Na on 9/25____	IV antibiotics, O2, Nebs, IV steroids	Diagnosis: Pneumonia Hx: Back pain, MI, COPD, CVA
Review date				
Review date				

Potential queries to consider	**Follow-up**
Na level 121 with repeat level ordered. Corresponding diagnosis?	
Lung sounds wheezes, Nebs, IV steroids, Hx COPD. Acute or normal state or ____?	

FIGURE 4.3
Sample CDS worksheet with example.

document verbal queries, which may have occurred between the physician and CDS. According to the American Health Information Management Association (AHIMA, 2008), the query form usually includes the following information: the patient's name, date of admission, account and medical record number, the date, name, and reference of who originated the question and a query with supporting clinical evidence and information from the chart. As discussed with the CDS worksheet, the query form may be handwritten or computer-generated. Some of the headings may be automatically populated if using a computerized form, or the CDS may have to handwrite the demographic information. See Figure 4.4.

According to the AHIMA (2008), there are specific reasons to query physicians. These include legibility, completeness, clarity, consistency, and

Name **Birth date**	**Admit date**	**Medical record number**	**Account number**
Initial DRG	**Discharge date**	**Final DRG**	**Coder's initials**
Date	**Query**	**CDS Name** **Extension**	**Response**

FIGURE 4.4
Sample query form.

precision. An *illegible* record is not only difficult for the CDS to read, but if the chart is chosen for an audit, especially with the implementation of recovery audit contractors (RACs), it will also be difficult to explain the thought processes behind the documentation, not to mention potential legal ramifications. An example of an illegible record may be when two or more qualified people cannot read either all or part of the documentation. This can occur because of poor handwriting, scrawls, scribbling, or unapproved abbreviations. The use of an electronic medical record may reduce this problem because the documentation is presented via a computerized system instead of a handwritten note.

Incompleteness may be demonstrated when there is an abnormal diagnostic finding but no documentation to support the implication or importance of the finding. An example may be the CDS notes on chart review that the patient's sodium level is abnormal at 124, with a normal range of 135–145 mEq/L (Medical Encyclopedia, n.d.). The physician has ordered to "repeat the sodium level in the morning"; however, there is no documentation of the sodium level, supporting condition, or diagnosis. This lack of acknowledgement demonstrates an incomplete record.

Clarification can be an issue when the diagnosis is vague without a reason or source of the condition. Some conditions may begin as a symptom when the doctor initially orders diagnostic tests for the patient to determine the diagnosis; however, leaving the final diagnosis as a symptom does not support a clear understanding of the condition. Some diagnoses that may need clarification are the etiology of dyspnea, chest pain, abdominal pain, nausea and vomiting, or altered mental status. These diagnoses may be clarified to a more specific cause after testing and should be documented in the patient record.

Another criterion to query is *inconsistency* in documentation. This initially may be seen when a person is admitted and the diagnosis has yet to be determined. Initially the physician may document "rule out pneumonia versus acute bronchitis." As the diagnostic results are reviewed and the clinical condition improves with appropriate treatment, a final diagnosis should be made. However, if pneumonia is documented in one entry of the progress notes and bronchitis in another, then pneumonia again, then bronchitis, the inconsistent documentation needs to be clarified. This type of inconsistency may also happen when more than one provider is documenting the diagnosis.

An example of lack of *precision* is when the diagnosis could be clarified beyond a general term. Meticulous documentation supports an accurate picture of the patient. A person may have pneumonia, but the diagnosis is more precise if the doctor documents methicillin-resistant *Staphylococcus aureus* (MRSA) pneumonia. This diagnosis supports the use of specific antibiotics and isolation precautions. In addition, the MRSA pneumonia has an expected longer LOS than simple pneumonia.

Although the query form is used for specific reasons to query the physician, it may also provide an opportunity for communication with nurses and case managers. As the CDS reviews the chart and discusses the findings with the nurse, information on the query form may remind the nurse of some additional concerns or documentation that is needed. For example, sharing with the nurse that the bronchoscopy culture grew MRSA but there is no clarification of the type of pneumonia documented, the query form provides a visual reminder for the nurse to notify the physician when she sees it written. In addition, the query form also contains the initial DRG. For case managers who review the chart, this information can help them see what the CDS has determined the initial working DRG to be.

Query Criteria

The aforementioned five criteria provide a guide to determine when to query a physician. However, how the query is stated has another set of criteria. According to AHIMA (2008), "the query should not sound presumptive, directing, prodding, probing, or as though the provider is being led to make an assumption." The queries should not be leading but provide open-ended questions or multiple choices. This may seem difficult for the CDS to word the query while trying not to lead the physician to a specific answer. However, stating the objective information retrieved from the patient's current record and giving the physician potential choices, including a choice of "other" or "unable to determine," allows the physician to choose what he or she feels are the appropriate diagnoses for the patient. For example, when querying the physician for a patient's type of congestive heart failure (CHF), multiple choices are listed on the query form, including acute systolic CHF, chronic systolic CHF, acute diastolic CHF, chronic diastolic CHF, acute systolic and diastolic CHF, other ________________________, or unable to determine. The question is stated on the query form with the CDS's name and contact information. This informs the physician which CDS wrote the query. In the response section the CDS can document where the physician has written his or her response in the chart. See Figure 4.5.

Name Mark Williams **Birth date** 7/20/28	**Admit date** 1/2/09	**Medical record number** M077432	**Account number** F25332345
Initial DRG 195	**Discharge date**	**Final DRG**	**Coder's initials**
Date	**Query**	**CDS Name Extension**	**Response**
1/4/09	Dr. Jans: The BNP CHF is 1257. The patient is receiving IV furosemide and had the carvedilol increased. The recent echocardiogram shows an ejection fraction of 25%. See report. CHF is documented in the progress notes. Please specify the type of CHF you are treating in your notes: Acute systolic CHF Chronic systolic CHF Acute diastolic CHF Chronic diastolic CHF Acute systolic and diastolic CHF Other_______________ Or unable to determine	Andrea x 2100	See physician progress notes on 1/5/09

FIGURE 4.5
Sample query form with example.

Using the same verbiage that is written in the chart provides information in the chart writer's own words. If the documentation says, "The patient has an open area on the foot," then the CDS should use this same verbiage in the query when asking about the type and etiology of the "open area." To help see other situations or possibilities for querying the physician, see Scenario 4.1 for further examples of potential accurate documentation.

SCENARIO 4.1

Scenario One

A 63-year-old male patient is admitted from the physician's office with blood urea nitrogen (BUN) of 108 mg/dL and serum creatinine of 3.9 mg/dL (normal results for BUN, 7–20 mg/dL; for serum creatinine, 0.8–1.4 mg/dL per MedlinePlus Medical Encyclopedia, n.d.). His urine is concentrated, and mucous membranes are dry. The physician orders IV fluids, and the initial creatinine improves from 3.9 mg/dL to 1.2 mg/dL after treatment. The initial BUN of 108 mg/dL improves to 54 mg/dL. The physician documents the patient was dehydrated. (The patient's normal baseline creatinine is 1.4 mg/dL.) Although the patient was dehydrated, the documentation does not represent the renal involvement. A query could be written for a more precise diagnosis. "Doctor, the patient had an improvement in the BUN from 108 to 54 and the creatinine from 3.9 to 1.2 with IV fluids. From the patient's baseline renal status, is there a more precise diagnosis representing the patient's condition? Dehydration, dehydration with acute renal failure, acute or chronic renal failure, or ____________________?" This query gives the physician some potential choices including a "fill in the blank." Although the CDS may think one of these is the corresponding diagnosis for the condition, the physician weighs the lab results with the clinical picture of the patient and treatment plan and may determine a different diagnosis. This is why a fill-in-the-blank line is appropriate for the query form. However, unless the query form is a permanent part of the chart, the physician still must document the medical record.

Scenario Two

A 75-year-old female patient is admitted through the emergency room with bloody, mucous stools, nausea, and vomiting. The physician documents the patient has probable gastroenteritis versus gastrointestinal bleeding. The patient's hemoglobin decreases from 11.4 gm/dL to 7.7 gm/dL. The patient has a colonoscopy, and stool aspirate is positive for *Clostridium difficile* bacteria. The patient is treated with blood transfusions, vancomycin, and IV fluids. Documenting the etiology of the gastroenteritis as *C. difficile* colitis would give a more accurate picture of the patient's gastroenteritis. In addition, because of the decrease in hemoglobin, which required blood transfusions, the physician should specify a diagnosis for the low hemoglobin. The physician initially documents "↓ hgb"; however, this abbreviation cannot be coded as a diagnosis. The physician is queried regarding a potential corresponding diagnosis. "Doctor, you noted ↓ hgb; however, this is not a term, condition, or diagnosis that can be coded. Please clarify in your notes the corresponding diagnosis for ↓ hgb." The physician documents anemia but does not specify the etiology of the anemia, or whether the anemia is acute or chronic. A subsequent query is written. "Doctor, anemia is noted in the progress notes; however, with the supporting evidence of the decreased hemoglobin, blood transfusions, positive stool specimen for *C. difficile*, and vancomycin ordered, please specify the etiology of the anemia. In addition, is the anemia acute, chronic, acute and chronic, or ____________________?" Another query may include the following for clarification, "The initial progress notes have probable gastroenteritis versus gastrointestinal bleeding. Please clarify if the patient has either or both of these diagnoses or ____________________." Later, the physician adds *C. difficile* colitis with acute blood-loss anemia in the progress notes to capture the true picture of the patient's condition.

Scenario Three

A 59-year-old female patient is admitted through the emergency room by ambulance with a diagnosis of respiratory distress. The patient has severe dyspnea with respirations of 32 per minute and is unable to speak in complete sentences. Arterial blood gases (ABGs) are obtained, which reveal acidosis with a pH of 7.18, an elevated $PaCO_2$ of 87 mm Hg, a decreased PaO_2 of 55 mm Hg, and elevated bicarbonate of 32 mEq/L. The patient is placed on oxygen with bilevel positive airway pressure (BiPAP), given nebulizer treatments and intravenous medications, and admitted to the intensive care unit. Frequent assessments and repeat ABGs reveal an improvement in the patient's condition. While the patient was in distress, the ABGs, clinical picture, and treatment plan correspond with a more precise diagnosis than respiratory distress. A query is written for the physician with the supporting evidence of the patient's critical condition, including the abnormal ABGs, BiPAP, intensive treatment, and monitoring. After reviewing the presenting information on the query form, the physician documents the patient had acute respiratory failure. Documenting the acute respiratory failure demonstrates the more appropriate diagnosis for this patient's condition and utilization of resources.

Presenting the clinical information and treatments for the above conditions provides the physician with the supporting information to document the accurate picture of the patient. From here, it is up to the physician to diagnose and document according to his or her medical expertise.

The query process is not about changing the DRG but rather about accurate documentation to support the true clinical picture of the patient's condition and treatments. Although some vendors may focus on the change of the DRG, accurate documentation of the patient's condition should be the priority. Accurate documentation provides for a complete medical record. According to Standard RC.02.01.01 of The Joint Commission on Accreditation of Healthcare Organizations, the patient's medical record should contain "information that reflects the [patient's] care, treatment, and services" (2009, p. 39). This supports the importance of an accurate record. Understanding the importance of accurate documentation is crucial to the success of the CDS program and care of the patient.

Technology

With today's technology, paperless systems, including electronic medical records (EMRs), can enhance the process or make it more challenging. Although the EMR may appear to have an easy point-and-click approach to documentation, if the choices are not accurate or adequate, the documentation may be insufficient to create the most accurate picture of the patient. In addition, the choices may not have the correct verbiage that the coder needs when coding a chart. For example, the choice may be "congestion," but the term is vague and would need further clarification.

If the choices were more comprehensive, the physician could choose the one that most accurately describes the type of congestion, the etiology, or the corresponding diagnosis. Because these choices should coincide with the terms needed for the coding world, the CDS can give valuable input when creating the physician's documentation piece of the EMR. The CDS can integrate his or her knowledge with the information technology (IT) department or computer department when creating templates or choices for documentation. Whereas the IT department understands the technical component of the system, the CDS understands what constitutes a complete diagnosis. Although providing the physician with a few choices for a diagnosis may seem adequate, it does not support accurate documentation.

In addition, involving the IT department can help when developing tools or forms for the CDS role. The IT department can incorporate the information needed from the CDS worksheet and query forms into a computerized format. Moreover, a computerized system can help with data collection. For those who use a paper system, using a colored query form can help it stand out in the chart. The placement of the form should be in a user-friendly place for the physician. If the physician cannot find the form, chances are it will get lost in the shuffle of papers and be ignored.

Systematic Review Method

The CDS role does not end with asking a question on the query form. These are only the beginning steps in the process. From here, the CDS must develop a systematic method for following up on queries and determining when the next review should occur. Because lengths of stay are potentially short, one should plan for the next review in 1–2 days. For someone who works Monday through Friday, the CDS may decide to do all reviews on Mondays, Wednesdays, and Fridays. On Tuesdays and Thursdays, the CDS will review any new patients plus follow up on any queries he or she had from the previous days. However, in a healthcare setting, we work with people and not objects. The hospital is a 24/7 world where census may fluctuate within hours, changing any planned schedule 180 degrees. This requires flexibility in the routine. In addition, just because the query sheet is in the chart does not mean the physician will read it or respond. Verbal discussions have become part of the concurrent review. However, just as written queries cannot be leading, neither can verbal ones. Not every query needs to be followed with a discussion. Being visible for the physician provides a reminder that the query form is in the chart. In addition, being available at the time of physician rounds provides an opportunity for any questions.

After the physician has responded to a query, it is important to document a response on the query form. This may be in the form of a checkmark noting that the query has been addressed or the location of the response with a corresponding date. This will facilitate coding the final chart because the coders can see what has already been addressed and where the information is located in the chart. However, one needs to remember the physician must document in the medical record for the coders to code the diagnosis or condition. At times, a physician may write directly on the query form; however, unless the form is a permanent part of the chart, the information needs to also be documented in the chart.

Physician Response Concerns

A physician may not always respond to written or verbal queries or be unwilling to participate in a discussion with the CDS. One must evaluate potential reasons for the lack of response. Maybe the query is unclear or illegible or the diagnosis cannot yet be determined. Communication is essential to the process. This should not be a cat and mouse game but rather an effort to do the right thing as the team works together for accuracy in documentation. Having open discussions while listening to each other's perspectives can facilitate the process. However, if the CDS has attempted to communicate with the physician without success, then a physician liaison may be helpful. The physician liaison should understand the CDS role and its purpose along with being a respected, knowledgeable physician with admirable communication skills.

The Working DRG Assignment and Impacts

After the CDS reviews the chart, he or she determines the working DRG and places this on the query form. In addition to knowing the patient's potential DRG, which correlates with the LOS, this will help with tracking progress and data collection. Each time the CDS reviews the chart, he or she should determine whether the working DRG has changed. If the coders are concurrently coding the chart, the CDS and coders should communicate any discrepancies they have in the DRG assignment. When the CDS obtains additional documentation, he or she should update the assigned working DRG concurrently. This is especially important for other departments that monitor LOS according to the DRG, such as case management. When the case management staff sees the working DRG on the query form has changed, they can assess whether the LOS also changed. In addition, the working DRG may have changed from one not affected by the postacute transfer policy to one that is (see Chapter 3).

Understanding what affects each DRG assignment is another aspect of the CDS role. Because some complications and comorbid conditions (CCs) and major CCs (MCCs) affect some of the DRGs but not all, the CDS should be familiar with differences in the DRGs. Knowing the different CCs and MCCs is one part of understanding the DRG assignment. In addition, the CDS should have a process to know what CCs and MCCs affected the DRG from each specific chart. Knowing this will help identify whether the query on the form affected the DRG from the documentation or whether the DRG would have changed from another diagnosis captured in the medical record. An example would be if the patient has CHF, and the query was in regard to the low sodium level of 124. The physician may document the corresponding diagnosis of hyponatremia, which would give the DRG assignment a CC. However, if the physician also documented in the chart another diagnosis, such as a urinary tract infection (UTI), the DRG would have already had the CC included. In this case, the query for the low sodium did not have an impact on the DRG assignment. However, the diagnosis of the hyponatremia does provide a more accurate picture of the clinical situation and affects the severity of illness for the patient. All three diagnoses of CHF, UTI, and hyponatremia give a more complete picture of the patient. However, the CHF could be made even more specific by inquiring about the type of CHF. Although again this does not affect the DRG assignment, more accurate documentation of the clinical condition would be provided.

However, if the query response resulted in a different DRG assignment, the CDS would compare what the DRG assignment would be before the query impact with what it is after the impact. If the DRG changed from a 293, heart failure and shock without a CC/MCC, to 292, heart failure and shock with CC, the relative weight (RW) would increase from 0.7220 to 1.0069 (CMS, Table 5—List of MS-DRGs of the Federal Register, 2008).

This is a difference of 0.2849, which can be converted to a financial impact. As discussed in Chapter 3, if the hospital's reimbursement was $5,000 per 1.0 RW, the impact would be $1,424.50.

0.2849 (change in RW) × $5,000 (reimbursement rate) = $1,424.50

This difference is part of the reimbursement considered necessary for the additional resources to care for the patient with the higher weighted DRG. In addition, the geometric mean LOS would increase from 3.1 days to 4.1 days, which is potentially needed to treat the CC.

After the patient is discharged, the query form goes with the chart to the medical records department, where the coders can code the entire chart. Ideally, all the queries should be addressed while the patient is still in the hospital. However, because this is not always realistic, queries that have not been answered should be addressed retrospectively. How this happens depends on the process the organization has put in place. The coder may be responsible for sending the chart to the physician for further documentation, or the CDS may address the query retrospectively with the physician before the chart is completed. After the documentation and chart are completed, the coder documents on the query form the final DRG and returns the sheet to the CDS. This allows the CDS to compare the initial working DRG with any changes in the DRG to the final DRG. The accuracy in documentation should support the changes in the DRG. By knowing the DRG, one should be able to find the supporting documentation in the chart.

An Internal Audit

In addition to the coders' role in finalizing the chart for billing, the coders may also provide an informal audit of the CDS's queries. When the coders are coding the chart, they may perform this audit. Or the coders may randomly pull a set number of charts each month or a percentage depending on the number of charts reviewed every month. They compare the chart information with the queries and the documentation. Performing an audit while the chart is being coded allows the CDS and coder to have a discussion concerning discrepancies before the chart is finalized. This provides opportunities for discussion and learning as concerns regarding the chart audit can be discussed while the information is fresh in each staff member's mind. During the audit, the coders can assess whether the queries are leading. In addition, they can assess whether the query meets one of the five reasons to query according to the AHIMA (2008): "legibility ... completeness ... clarity ... consistency ... (and) ... precision." Communication between the coders and CDS is important because they can share knowledge from both the clinical and coding viewpoints.

Completing the Loop

After the chart is coded and billed, it is not finished. A process should be established to ensure any payment denials are sent back to the appropriate individual. The revenue cycle process team may include the precertification department, the case managers, the CDS, the coders, and the billing office. Other members may need to be added ad hoc as situations arise. If the payment denial is associated with precertification, the utilization review or case management department should be informed. If the denial is associated with documentation, the CDS and physician should be involved. Providing this loop back to the original sources not only can help appeal denials, it can also prevent further issues. In addition, these opportunities can be used for future education.

DATA COLLECTION AND CONSIDERATIONS

Data collection can help support the CDS's role while providing trends for potential changes. Some of the data collection can be obtained from the query forms. Some areas to measure include the number of charts reviewed, the number of concurrent queries, the number of retrospective queries, the DRG change impacts, and the physician responses to queries. For example, if there are 500 discharges in the month, how many discharged charts were reviewed: 400 or 80%, 450 or 90%, or 500 or 100%? What is the organization's target for the number reviewed: 90%, 100%? Also, if 500 charts were reviewed, how many total queries were on all the charts: 1,850, 1,925, 2,000? Of the total queries, how many were concurrent while the patient was still admitted in the hospital versus how many were retrospective queries after the patient was discharged? For example, if 2,000 queries were done per month and 1,500 were concurrent, then

75% of the queries occurred while the patient was still in the hospital. This would mean 25% happened after the patient was discharged. Is this an acceptable amount for the organization, or should more queries be done concurrently? Another measure might be how many charts had DRG changes related to the queries? If 450 charts were reviewed and 125 had DRG changes, this would mean approximately 28% of the charts had DRG impacts from the queries. What was the total amount of change in the RW from all the DRG changes? This change in RW can be converted to a financial impact by multiplying the total change in the RW by the organization's reimbursement rate. If information is entered into a computer, a spreadsheet or graph can be created to monitor for trends or patterns. See Table 4.1. Although these data may be fictitious, they allow one to monitor for trends such as the percentage of concurrent queries increased and retrospective queries decreased. This may potentially mean more CDS and physician collaboration occurs while the patient is still in the hospital.

After collecting data and monitoring patterns, benchmarks should be established along with measurable goals. Although one may think 100% should be the target for all areas, this may not appropriate. For example,

TABLE 4.1

Example Data Spreadsheet

	Jan	Feb	Mar	Apr
# Total discharge charts	500	480	520	475
# Charts reviewed	450	457	475	460
% Charts reviewed	90	95	91	97
# Total queries	2,000	1,945	2,020	1,900
# Concurrent queries	1,500	1,600	1,710	1,700
% Concurrent queries	75	82	85	89
# Retrospective queries	500	345	310	200
% Retrospective queries	25	18	15	11
% Physician response to queries	68	79	91	91
% Physician agreement with queries	42	56	68	62
# Charts with DRG changes	125	95	127	90
% Charts with DRG changes	28	21	27	20
Total RW change	43.24	40.56	44.21	39.6
Financial impact	$216,200	$202,800	$221,050	$198,000

responding to a query and agreeing with a query are two separate issues. The physician should respond to 100% of the queries, but he or she may not agree 100% of the time with them. The physician should use his or her knowledge and clinical judgment when responding to queries. However, if there is a low percentage of agreement, then the process should be evaluated. Is there an internal audit established for the appropriateness of queries? Are there communication barriers impeding the CDS and physician's interactions? Potential concerns or negative patterns should be evaluated and adjustments made accordingly.

However, one must remember the data are not independent of other factors. Other influences may be the number and type of surgical procedures and patient census. If physician responses to the queries decrease, one must evaluate potential reasons for the decline. Has communication decreased? Are physicians having patient rounds at a different time than when the CDS is available for discussion? Has the query process changed? Are the queries clear and based on clinical information in the chart? Has the workload increased? These may affect physician responses and should be evaluated and acted on as needed.

After collecting data, establishing benchmarks, monitoring for patterns, and making goals, the results should be presented to the fiscal department and administration. Both of these departments should be aware and understand the impact of accurate documentation. However, although one may focus on the financial impact of DRG, the emphasis should still remain on the accuracy of documentation. When the patient's condition is accurately documented, the financial and quality pieces should fall into place. For example, if everything is documented appropriately, one should be able to know whether the conditions were present on admission (POA) versus hospital-acquired conditions (HACs). The patient's severity of illness will coincide with the documentation because the true picture capturing all appropriate diagnoses is documented and coded. If a payment denial occurs on the claim, the chart should already have the supporting documentation for the appeal process.

Other departments that may be interested in the data may also be those affected by the documentation, DRGs, and LOS. A committee may be formed by these departments, including case management or utilization review staff, the inpatient coding department, the CDSs, a physician liaison or advisor, the quality department, and associated directors. The focus and frequency of the meeting depend on the goals and mission of the committee. This group may focus on the various impacts, challenges, and potential areas that need to be addressed. Educational opportunities should be considered depending on the needs of the committee. Accurate documentation does not affect only one area. Considering the importance of accurate documentation from other perspectives mentioned in Chapter 3, such as RAC, POA, and HAC, the CDS role continues to be an asset for the organization.

CDS ROLE ALLOCATIONS AND JOB DESCRIPTION

When developing a clinical documentation program, one needs to consider the role functions and potential impacts when writing the job description. The job description may include chart review; working DRG assignment; ongoing collaboration with physicians, nurses, coders, and other healthcare disciplines; data collection; educational presentations; policy and process development; and continued CDS education. The role should be divided into categories, with potential work time or percentages assigned for each area. One may consider concurrent chart review, DRG assignment, and collaboration as the primary roles and allocate 70% of the time for this section. Data collection and reports might be given 10%. Five percent of the time might be allowed for providing education through formal presentations. Five percent may focus on policy development, informal staff education, and workflow processes. The remaining 10% might be dedicated to additional learning opportunities for the CDS's education. This allows the CDS to invest in his or her role by staying current with documentation, coding, and clinical aspects of disease processes and treatments.

CDS SUPPORT

Another aspect to consider is adding a physician advisor or champion. This person can help support the process as he or she interacts with other physicians when the need arises. For example, if the CDS has queried the physician on a particular chart and the physician does not respond even after multiple attempts and conversation, the CDS may need to involve the physician advisor. After discussing the case with the CDS, the physician advisor can speak with the physician on the case. This physician-to-physician conversation may help with a positive response. Again, this does not mean the physician on the case must agree with the physician advisor. However, it provides an opportunity to have the physicians discuss the case and determine whether there is an opportunity for more accurate documentation of the clinical picture.

The physician champion can help with educational presentations to bring the information forward from a physician's perspective. The physician advisor must also have commendable communication skills, a basic understanding of DRGs and the CDS role, and established clinical knowledge. Respect from colleagues regarding the advisor's behaviorisms and medical knowledge is vital for the success of the role. The CDS and physician advisor should establish scheduled meetings to ensure the progress of the program. This is especially crucial in the early stages of the program because not all physicians and other staff may be on board in terms of their understanding of the importance of the program. They may need to be shown how the program benefits them. How does accurate documentation affect them? An explanation of terms such as *case mix*, *RW*, and *severity of illness* may be beneficial. In addition, as discussed in Chapter 3, with the RAC program going nationwide, documentation is crucial to help justify the patient's true clinical picture and the treatment. The physician advisor may be part of other collaborative teams, such as the interdisciplinary care team and the organization's RAC committee. This collaborative approach with the various disciplines allows the group to view its purpose from a holistic perspective.

Finally, we must mention the importance of administrative support. A CDS program may have all the right people doing the right job, but without the support of administration, the program may fail. Or minimally the program will not succeed to its fullest potential. Administration needs to understand the purpose and the impact of the program because the CDS program should be presented to the organization's governing board. The board needs to understand how the program and collaboration affect the organization in a variety of ways, including the financial and quality impacts mentioned in Chapter 3. An educational session should be given to the board to help them understand the program. Because the governing board may not understand the clinical significance of accurate documentation, the information should be presented in a clear format while not using extensive clinical terms but rather focusing on the basic concepts of the program. Visuals such as graphs and spreadsheets with basic terms and definitions can help when presenting the program. In addition, providing monthly data can give the administrative board concrete information on how the program affects the organization.

SUMMARY

The CDS has the opportunity to promote accurate documentation by concurrently reviewing the clinical information and querying physicians. In turn, this opportunity promotes accurate coding as the information is already documented in the chart for the coders. The CDS program involves a systematic process to review the clinical information and chart documentation, write physician queries, and collaborate with other healthcare staff, such as coders, nurses, and case management workers. Data collection is part of the CDS process as trends and patterns can be monitored, including the number of queries, physician response rate, and DRG changes. Having support from administration is crucial to the program's success. In addition, a physician advisor is beneficial, as he or she can collaborate with the CDS and other physicians. The emerging CDS role supports accurate documentation with a real-time approach and can be a resource in the forever-changing healthcare maze.

REFERENCES

AHIMA. 2008. Managing an effective query process. American Health Information Management Association. http://library.ahima.org/xpedio/idcplg?IdcService=GET_HIGHLIGHT_INFO&QueryText=%28managing+an+effective+query+process%29%3cand%3e%28xPublishSite%3csubstring%3e%60BoK%60%29&SortField=xPubDate&SortOrder=Desc&dDocName=bok1_040394&HighlightType=HtmlHighlight&dWebExtension=hcsp (accessed January 1, 2009).

Centers for Medicare and Medicaid Services. 2008. Table 5—List of MS-DRGs, relative weighting factors, and geometric & arithmetic mean length of stay. FY 2009 final rule. *Federal Register* 73:161.

Coding Clinic. 2005. Reporting additional diagnoses coding guidelines. First quarter 2005.

The Joint Commission on Accreditation of Healthcare Organizations. 2009. Accreditation Program Hospital. Record of care, treatment, and services. p. 39.

Medical Encyclopedia. n.d. MedlinePlus. http://www.nlm.nih.gov/medlineplus/ency/article/003481.htm (accessed January 3, 2009).

5

Clinical Documentation Specialist and Education

Choosing the right person for the clinical documentation specialist (CDS) role is essential for the success of the program. A nurse with a strong, diverse clinical background and a basic understanding of coding is encouraged for this position. In addition, exceptional communication skills are vital because the CDS needs to collaborate with many disciplines in the healthcare environment. Although one may learn the idiosyncrasies of the use of specific forms, technical equipment, processes, and coding, the person's clinical knowledge and ability to build an alliance with others are crucial for the position. Interpersonal communication skills should be considered when evaluating a person for the role. In addition to commendable communication skills and collaboration experience, the position also requires critical thinking, responsibility, and follow-through, along with the ability to keep current with changes in regulations.

CDS TRAINING

Good CDS training is imperative because the CDS must understand various aspects of the role and its impacts. However, not only is choosing the right new CDS for the role important, so is choosing the right preceptor. The preceptor should be knowledgeable of the educational material and the CDS process but also needs to be a good mentor. The preceptor needs to not only teach the new CDS but also integrate the person into the role. The preceptor should introduce the new CDS to other members of the group, which may include other CDSs, coders, and the physician advisor. In addition, the new CDS should be introduced to physicians, nurses, and other healthcare workers. This promotes a positive atmosphere as the new CDS is welcomed and familiarized with others and also promotes collaboration between the new CDS and others.

Another aspect that is not always obvious but should be considered when training someone is an understanding of the person's learning style. As with any learning process, one should begin with assessing the person's learning style. A discussion about how the person has learned in the past may be beneficial. Is the person an auditory learner who benefits more from hearing the information? Is the person a visual learner who comprehends information by reading? Or is the person a tactile learner who needs to be able to have hands-on application? Although all three attributes may be used in the orientation, understanding the person's basic learning style can facilitate the learning process. From here, the orientation plan can be individualized to include the learner's preferred style. The auditory person may benefit from more discussions about the CDS process and material, whereas the visual learner may desire to read the material instead of listening to lengthy discussions or presentations of the material. The tactile learner may prefer to work "hands on" to apply the information as he or she learns it. For some, a combination of all three styles may be required. Although the basic orientation process should be maintained, altering the program to fit the learner's style may help the new CDS learn the role.

Clinical Knowledge and Experience

After the preceptor has discussed the new CDS's learning style, a specific orientation plan should be created. The training begins with assessing the CDS's clinical knowledge and previous experience. Where has the person worked: hospital, office, or another type of facility? What type of clinical experience has he or she had: medical, oncology, critical care? How many years has the person worked in each different area? The clinical knowledge the CDS will need to have may depend on whether a unit-based or physician-based model is used. If the CDS will remain on specific units, he or she can focus on the disease processes that correlate with the specific type of unit. If the CDS will follow specific physicians, he or she needs to know diseases or conditions of the physician's patient population. For a general approach, the CDS should understand the disease processes of the top 10 diagnosis-related groups (DRGs) and comorbid conditions for the physician group or unit.

Coding and DRG Terms

Next, one should evaluate the CDS's understanding of coding and the DRG system. Begin with providing material on various terms such as CC, MCC, RW, principal diagnosis, LOS, DRG, HAC, POA, observation, inpatient status, and medical necessity. These terms are crucial for understanding the CDS role (see Chapter 3). Not only should the definition of the terms be explained, examples of how the terms apply to the role should also be given. However, the CDS should not focus on memorizing words and definitions but rather be able to apply them. Providing the relevance of the term and giving examples may help the new CDS learn them faster. For example, a CC is a complication or comorbid condition that is not the primary diagnosis. A CC may be demonstrated in a patient who is admitted with pneumonia and also has a urinary tract infection (UTI). The CC is the UTI. If one gives an example of a CC (the UTI), it may help the CDS learn more what the term means than just the definition. However, there are many different diagnoses listed as CCs, and memorizing the list could be overwhelming. If one is taught the basic concept of what the term means and how it relates to other terms such as a DRG, the CDS can have a resource list of all the different CCs available, instead of memorizing them. This would be applicable for other acronyms such as MCC (major complication or comorbid condition) and HAC (hospital-acquired condition). The new CDS should spend his or her time learning and applying the concept instead of memorizing all the corresponding diagnoses or conditions that accompany the acronym.

In addition, if one has limited knowledge about coding and the related terms, the new CDS should spend time with a coder to be trained on the various aspects of coding, including choosing the principal diagnosis, diagnosis coding, procedural coding, and sequencing. Although the CDS may not be a certified coder for this role, the knowledge is essential in understanding how the role functions. If the organization uses a computerized coding system, the CDS should spend time learning how the system works regarding International Statistical Classification of Diseases and Related Health Problems (ICD)-9 Clinical Modification (CM) codes or the future ICD-10 codes and DRGs. In addition, the CDS should review the official guidelines for coding and have access to updates as they occur.

The Query Process

Next steps include understanding the query process. What are the five reasons to query a physician? What constitutes a compliant query (see Chapter 4)? Providing examples by using realistic situations may be beneficial. The next phase is having the new CDS spend time with an experienced CDS to learn more of the process, including systematic chart review, query writing, and physician interactions. If the organization uses electronic medical records and CDS software, these should be incorporated into the training.

Initially, start with observation and progress according to the learner's response and understanding. However, remember that even when one appears to understand, the mentor should be available to provide support, answer questions, examine query forms, and perform audits for compliance and accuracy. While the new CDS is learning the role, he or she should also be provided with information about financial, quality, and severity of illness impacts as they relate to accurate documentation. Reviewing reports in these areas can provide a better understanding of the impacts.

An orientation outline and list of learning objectives can help the new CDS learn the role while at the same time providing guidance of key areas for the preceptor. The orientation table is designed to include the date and activity the new CDS should learn in his or her training. On the table, an area is provided for the preceptor's name or initials, along with the new CDS's response to the activity. The new CDS's response to the activity should be documented in the response column. If the CDS has completed the activity and no further education or training is required, the date of completion should be documented. However, if more training is required, a further action plan should be listed. See Figure 5.1 for an example orientation activity table and Figure 5.2 for the corresponding CDS orientation learning objectives.

Date	Activity/ competency The new CDS will:	Preceptor	Response	Further education required (if further education is required, address action)	Completed
	Identify and verbalize the person's learning style: i.e., verbal, visual, tactile.				
	Explain the signs and symptoms, including diagnostics and treatments for common disease processes and conditions for top 10 DRGs and CCs.				
	Explain terms and application: i.e., CC, MCC, case mix, RW, principal diagnosis, additional diagnoses, DRG, HAC, POA, medical necessity, observation, inpatient, ICD-9 (or current diagnosis coding), MDC, geometric mean length of stay, severity of illness, quality core measures.				
	Explain basic coding rules: i.e., diagnosis coding, procedural coding, additional diagnoses, sequencing, undetermined diagnosis: i.e., "probable," "suspected," "possible," or "still to be ruled out."				
	Spend time with coder applying coding terms and rules. Provide reasons and components of a compliant query with examples. Provide examples of noncompliant queries.				
	Demonstrate chart review and coding using electronic coder or coding book material.				
	Explain financial, quality, severity of illness, and accurate documentation impacts and reports.				

FIGURE 5.1
CDS orientation table.

Date	Activity/competency The new CDS will:	Preceptor	Response	Further education required (if further education is required, address action)	Completed
	Spend time with CDS to learn CDS process, including systematic chart review, queries, and physician interactions (initially start with observation and progress according to the learner's response and understanding).				
	Differentiate between a verbal and written query.				
	Write compliant queries.				
	Demonstrate appropriate communication skills and collaborative interaction with physician, nurses, case managers, coders, and other healthcare disciplines.				
	Assimilate accurate documentation data, including query response rates, DRG accuracy, RWs, and severity of illness.				

FIGURE 5.1 **(continued)**

The new Clinical Documentation Specialist will:
1. Identify and verbalize preferred learning style
2. Understand the top 10 DRGs and CCs by • Verbalizing anatomy and pathophysiology • Verbalizing common signs and symptoms • Verbalizing corresponding diagnostics • Verbalizing common treatments
3. Explain the following terms and how they apply to the CDS role • CC • MCC • Case mix • RW • Principal diagnosis • Additional diagnoses • Comorbid conditions • DRG • HAC • POA • Medical necessity • Observation • Inpatient • ICD-9 (or current diagnosis coding) • MDC • Geometric mean LOS • Severity of illness • Quality core measures
4. Differentiate the basic coding rules by • Explaining and applying rules for diagnosis coding • Explaining and applying rules for procedural coding • Explaining and applying rules for sequencing • Explain coding rules for undetermined diagnosis; i.e., "probable," "suspected," or "still to be ruled out"
5. Compare and contrast qualities of compliant and noncompliant queries
6. Specify five reasons to query according to AHIMA
7. Construct examples using these five reasons to query
8. Differentiate between a written and verbal query
9. Explain the quality impacts of accurate documentation as it relates to core measure and severity of illness
10. Give examples of corresponding web sites for quality data reporting
11. Explain the financial impacts of accurate documentation as it applies to the terms listed in Section 3

FIGURE 5.2
CDS orientation learning objectives.

12.	Perform systematic chart reviews, and identify opportunities for accurate documentation
13.	Create queries applying the above information as it relates to accurate documentation
14.	Demonstrate constructive interactions with physicians
15.	Assimilate accurate documentation data, including query response rates, DRG accuracy, RWs, and severity of illness

FIGURE 5.2 (continued)

CDS CONTINUED EDUCATION

In addition to on-the-job training, the CDS needs to further his or her education to keep current with the many changes in healthcare that affect the CDS role. This may include the annual updates of DRGs, CC, MCC, and HAC. Continued education can be accomplished in a variety of ways. The CDS can find various reading material to support education. These may include articles on coding, disease processes, regulations, and revenue processes. Webinars and teleconferences provide another venue for continuing education. In addition, attending conferences and networking with other CDSs from other organizations not only provides educational opportunities but also rejuvenates the person. This helps prevent stagnation as the CDS exchanges ideas with others and revives the desire to excel in his or her role. Joining a professional association or organization can provide additional resources for education.

The CDS needs to keep current with changes in the clinical portion of the role, including new clinical practices and disease processes affecting his or her patient population. Even though the nurse working as a CDS may not apply technical skills, he or she must keep current to support his or her critical thinking. A CDS needs to know when to query for a certain disease process. If the CDS does not keep current with new medical terms, diagnostics, or disease processes, he or she may not realize physician's documentation needs further clarification. For example, if the CDS is not knowledgeable of the staging of chronic renal failure (chronic kidney disease) as it pertains to the glomerular filtration rate, he or she may not realize the disease can be staged. Or if the CDS is not aware of new pieces of equipment being used, he or she may not understand the significance of the equipment for providing further diagnostic information. Conversations with other nurses and physicians promote learning. This provides an opportunity to share knowledge as people working in different disciplines give their insight. Physicians have a wealth of information. Sharing this knowledge provides not only education but also an opportunity for physicians, nurses, case managers, documentation specialists, and people working in other healthcare disciplines to interact and collaborate.

CDS AND NURSING EDUCATION

Nurses may not realize what the CDS's role encompasses or how it affects them. The nurse may not realize the importance of what the CDS does. This is a good opportunity for education. The CDS can be part of the initial nursing orientation process or provide education at nursing staff meetings. The CDS can explain the basic functions of the role, including the chart review and physician documentation, but the nurses also need to know the CDS is part of the healthcare team and also looks at nurse's documentation. Nurses have been told the old adage, "If it was not documented, it was not done." However, nurses may wonder if anyone ever reads their documentation. Part of the education is to let nurses know their documentation is read and is important when portraying the patient's complete clinical picture. The CDS can explain how the nurse's documentation supports the patient's clinical picture and provides supporting information for requesting or clarifying physician documentation. In addition, the nurse's admission assessment may indicate whether the patient had signs and symptoms when admitted, which can help determine whether a diagnosis is present on admission (POA) or a HAC. The nurse may document on the admission assessment that the patient has wheezing throughout his lungs, dyspnea with exertion, a temperature of 100.1°F, and an oxygen saturation of 86% on 2 L/min of oxygen per nasal cannula. The patient may have been admitted for dehydration and UTI, but there is also evidence of respiratory compromise. The physician has ordered a chest x-ray, IV steroids, oxygen, and nebulizer treatments in addition to treatment for the dehydration. The physician documents that the patient has chronic obstructive pulmonary disease (COPD) but does not specify whether this is an acute exacerbation or the patient's normal state. Because the nurse documented a thorough picture of the patient's respiratory status on admission, the CDS refers to the admission notes, the treatment plan, and the physician's documentation of COPD to inquire about a more accurate diagnosis for the patient's respiratory condition. An example of this query might be "Doctor, the nurse's admission assessment notes wheezing throughout his lungs, dyspnea with exertion, a temperature of 100.1°F, and an oxygen saturation of 86% on 2 L/min of oxygen. The patient is on IV steroids and nebulizer treatments. COPD is documented in the chart. Please clarify with the patient's symptoms and treatment plan if the patient is having an acute exacerbation, if this is his normal status, or ____________?" After reviewing the query form and clinical data, the physician documents the patient has an acute exacerbation of COPD with acute bronchitis. This provides a more accurate picture of the patient's medical condition. In addition, the nurse's documentation supports the exacerbation of the COPD may have been present when the patient was admitted.

CDS AND PHYSICIAN EDUCATION

Nurses are not the only group to need education about the CDS role. Physicians should also be educated on the purpose of the role and the importance of the CDSs and physicians working together on accurate documentation in the patient record. However, physicians may not be receptive to the CDS role or purpose. In addition, if the physician does not know the CDS, he or she may wonder whether the CDS is knowledgeable and trustworthy. This trust may not happen immediately. However, the CDS should not assume the physician knows the CDS's background or experience. This became apparent when a physician asked whether I was a nurse after I commented that someone on the unit must have a gastrointestinal bleed because of a specific odor. I had assumed the physician knew my nursing background. However, because the physician had not been with the organization when I worked as a staff nurse, he did not know. This information alone should not be the deciding factor of whether I am competent in my role, but it gives the physician another perspective of my clinical experience when I query for supporting information of diagnoses.

An initial presentation should be given to physicians to educate them on the purpose of the CDS role and the process. This presentational format should allow for questions and answers. First, physicians should be given some historical background of why accurate documentation is important as it relates to quality and financial impacts, as well as how public reporting relates to the physician's care of his or her patients (see Chapter 3). When speaking with physicians, present information with concrete data. Give the physician examples, and explain how accurate documentation affects quality, financial, and public reporting as it relates to them. Also stress the importance of accurate documentation to support medical necessity. If the recovery audit contractors (RACs) review the chart and the documentation is accurate, it provides a stronger case for the patient being in the hospital and the care he or she received.

Physicians need to understand how documentation affects them. If a patient is admitted with documented urosepsis for a diagnosis, this codes to a UTI DRG. However, if the patient's true clinical picture and treatment are for sepsis, the physician should document accordingly. If not, when data are reviewed, it appears the physician used intense resources to treat a UTI when the patient was actually treated for sepsis. In addition, if the patient dies, it appears as though the patient died from a UTI instead of sepsis.

A physician may think he or she has documented appropriately but because the physician does not understand the coding world, the documentation may lack vital information. The CDS can describe to the physician how the basic coding process works. It is not simply someone sitting at a desk coming up with questions and entering diagnoses. There is a process the coders go through to determine the diagnosis code and DRG. What is the principal diagnosis? Are there sequencing rules to determine the principal diagnosis? Are there additional CC diagnoses? Did the patient have a surgical procedure (see Chapter 3)? However, even after demonstrating this process, the physician's thoughts may not be completely documented on paper. The physician may think he or she has documented methicillin-resistant *Staphylococcus aureus* (MRSA) pneumonia but instead only documented "culture MRSA" and did not link the note to the type of pneumonia. Or the physician may document "the creatinine is down, renal improving, continue IV fluids," but neither of these supports the actual verbiage of the diagnosis. What renal condition does the patient have? What is the etiology? Is it acute or chronic? Or is there another corresponding diagnosis? This appears to demonstrate a person's thought processes as the physician may think he or she has adequately documented the clinical picture and diagnosis, but there is not enough documentation to code the information. Although a clinical person may be able to comprehend what is happening and think the information is obvious, coding rules do not allow one to assume what is not documented.

One-on-one education and discussions are probably the best for concurrent education. The CDS should let physicians know he or she is willing to talk with them and provide a contact number in case they have questions when they have patient rounds at another time than when the CDS is present. Ideally, the CDS is available during rounds whenever possible. The CDS role should support the process, not hinder it. Although one cannot be there 24/7, the CDS should follow up with any questions the physicians have. Building trust is crucial when beginning the program and needs to be maintained by all parties.

Another opportunity for education is providing the physician with his or her work statistics, including query impacts, length of stay (LOS), and case mix. Sharing with the physician his or her individual results compared with overall results may create a clearer picture. This does not need to be a formal presentation but a snapshot of the physician's results. If his or her average LOS is 4.5 days and the organization's overall average is 3.7 days, this demonstrates the physician's LOS is longer than average. However, if the organization's overall case mix is 1.24 and the physician's is 1.66, then the score would correlate with his or her longer average LOS. Providing examples of differences in LOS and relative weights (RWs) according to various DRGs may be beneficial. However, the physician should also be informed that there are other areas that affect the case mix and LOS. How many of his or her patients have surgery? This generally corresponds to a higher case mix. However, presenting the information to the physician at least provides a general concept of his or her statistics.

Education in itself can have a collaborative approach. As the physician learns about accurate documentation, the CDS has the opportunity to ask questions to broaden his or her knowledge about disease processes. Moreover, these discussions should be considered from an educational opportunity viewpoint and not about questioning one's judgment on practice, approaches, or documentation. Both the CDS and physician need to understand this to prevent any misunderstanding or inhibit the lines of communication.

KEEPING CURRENT AND UNDERSTANDING CHANGE

Although one may think once physicians have learned the various aspects of documentation, the CDS role will be done; however, the coding world is frequently challenged to meet the demands of healthcare. The CDS should keep current with rules and regulations by accessing resources such as credible websites, professional associations or organizations, newsletters, fact sheets, and networking sessions. When new diagnoses and conditions emerge, codes must be created to reflect the changes. The ICD-9 codes, DRGs, RWs, and calculated LOSs are updated annually. To be compliant, one first must be knowledgeable of the changes and then apply them.

Work is underway to change the current ICD-9 CM system to the ICD-10 CM system. The ICD-10 CM system is constructed from the internationally used ICD-10 system, which was created by the World Health Organization (CMS Fact Sheet, 2009). ICD-10 CM coding provides even more opportunities for the CDS role because the codes are more complex than the ICD-9 CM system. According to Schneider (2009), the ICD-9 CM system has approximately 17,000 codes, whereas the ICD-10 system has 155,000 codes. Accurate documentation will be more crucial as the patient's condition can be specified to a more precise diagnosis using the ICD-10 CM system. Learning the ICD-10 CM codes and corresponding DRGs will require additional education for the CDS. In addition, the CDS will need to know how to correlate the coding system with the physician's documentation. As with any new system, a learning curve can be expected. Initial education sessions may be beneficial, but concurrent education and discussion will need to occur to support the change.

Applying Change

Kurt Lewin's model of change may facilitate the learning process as one develops an educational curriculum. Lewin's theory with the three concepts of unfreezing, changing, and refreezing can help one understand the process (Ervin, 2002). Various healthcare providers and staff initially had to learn the ICD-9 CM coding system and application. This did not happen overnight and certainly did not occur without some struggle or frustration. However, because the ICD-9 CM was required from many aspects, eventually everyone learned the system.

To apply the change process, healthcare providers will have to "unfreeze" numbers and the corresponding diagnoses they have ingrained in their memory. Although they may not desire to change or learn a new process, external influences may affect the need for change. These external influences may be regulatory bodies or financial consequences. For example, when the ICD-9 codes are updated to the ICD-10 system, if the organization does not learn and apply the changes, it may not have the capability to bill the payers with the updated codes. If the organization cannot bill, it will not be paid. This is one reason why staff will need to apply change. While staff is "unfreezing" previous knowledge, providing education of why the change is occurring can facilitate the process. Regarding the ICD-10 CM system, some of the reasons for the change include increasing the accuracy of diagnosis and allowing for global reporting of diseases while monitoring diseases and treatments internationally (CMS Fact Sheet, 2009). Understanding the reason for the change and including key players in the process can assist and support the conversion to the new system.

The second step of "change" is learning the ICD-10 CM system. This requires an action plan with education, support, and appropriate resources. Removing the previous system before implementing the new one would not be favorable for successful implementation. Because an external entity may control the implementation date of the new system, it is crucial that an adequate timeline is established that should include the "go-live" date. Providing available resources during the learning phase and the implementation phase can support the process. These resources may include ICD-10 reference materials and support staff members who understand the changes with the ICD-10 system. They should be available for the initial training and then provide continued mentoring during the transition phase.

During the "refreezing" stage, staff will need to commit to the use of the new process. If a regulatory body mandates the change and codes are rejected if the proper system is not used, there will be less chance of noncompliance. Noncompliance is not just a matter of not being willing to comply. It may mean the difference between following regulations and claims being accepted versus rejected. Because change is not always well received, it is important to understand the process, develop a plan, and support others in the process. This can provide a basis for understanding many future needs for education.

SUMMARY

The CDS role requires an intricate orientation plan as the position merges clinical, coding, quality, and financial areas into one role. Although the role may vary in different organizations, the CDS should have an understanding of these areas. Having a detailed plan with learning objectives and tools can facilitate the orientation process. In addition, the CDS must understand how his or her role relates to other disciplines and provide formal and informal education. Moreover, because healthcare is always changing, the CDS must keep current with developments in this dynamic field.

REFERENCES

CMS Fact Sheet. 2009. Details for: HHS modifies HIPPA code sets (ICD-10) and electronic transactions standards. Centers for Medicare and Medicaid Services. http://www.cms.hhs.gov/apps/media/press/factsheet.asp?Counter=3407&intNumPerPage=10&checkDate=&checkKey=&srchType=1&numDays=3500&srchOpt=0&srchData=&keywordType=All&chkNewsType=6&intPage=&showAll=&pYear=&year=&desc=&cboOrder=date (accessed January 15, 2009).

Ervin, N. 2002. *Advanced Community Health Nursing Practice*. Upper Saddle River, NJ: Prentice Hall.

Schneider, M. E. 2009. HHS finalizes plans for ICD-10 transition. January 16, 2009. http://www.mdconsult.com (accessed January 21, 2009).

6

Collaboration with Hospital Case Management

Healthcare has continued to evolve over the years. It is challenging to keep up with clinical information and technology, let alone the impacts of the financial and quality aspects of care. Organizations needed to ask themselves, "How can care be coordinated on a daily basis while managing the resources? Who is going to be able to incorporate the clinical, quality, and financial aspects while being a patient advocate?" Nurses are challenged with directly taking care of the patient and may not take care of the same patient every day. In addition, nurses may work at various times, including 8- or 12-hour shifts or only weekends. These aspects limit the nurses' continuity of coordinating the patient's care and managing resources on a daily basis. Because hospitals needed to manage their resources and coordinate care, case management has been brought into the picture.

Collaboration and coordination of patient care should occur throughout a patient's hospital stay. Although this may seem obvious, sometimes the obvious does not happen. From the time the patient enters the hospital's system, the staff can begin to build a cohesive team to take care of the patient and guide workers through a potentially challenging maze. Whether the patient is admitted directly or enters through the emergency room, healthcare workers can ensure a smooth flow and ease of care. Although not every patient may have the exact same course, opportunities arise to facilitate the process. Customer service is one of the biggest aspects that can influence a person's perception. The first encounter the patient has may set the scene for the rest of his or her stay. Anyone who comes in contact with the patient may be the deciding factor of whether that person feels the experience was positive or negative. This encounter may be with the admitting staff, the laboratory technician, the housekeeper, the dietician, the volunteer, the physician, or the unit nurses. Presenting an image in which all parties work together portrays a cohesive team. Some roles may overlap within an organization. However, it is not about territorial issues or who owns the role; the team must work together to maximize effectiveness and take care of the patient.

One member of this cohesive team involved with the patient either directly or indirectly throughout the hospital stay is the hospital case manager (CM). Case management is an enormous topic, and many books have already been written on the subject; this chapter will focus on the collaboration that can occur with the role of a hospital CM. This person has the challenge of meshing the patient's clinical, psychological, and social information and discharge plan with the payer's requirements and the length of stay. The CM also is a patient advocate and may help with patient education.

CASE MANAGEMENT LEGAL AND QUALITY CONSIDERATIONS

The hospital CM must understand the quality and legal components of the role. The CM also must understand the regulations and laws that are important to the case management role. These may vary in different states, and the CM should be knowledgeable about the laws in his or her area. Quality components may include the quality indicators as discussed in Chapter 3. If the quality indicators are incorporated into the patient care guidelines, the CMs should monitor to ensure the guidelines and quality indicators are followed. For example, if a patient is admitted with congestive heart failure (CHF), is the corresponding guideline being used? In addition, one of the quality indicators for CHF patients is assessing the left ventricular (LV) function. The CM should monitor whether there is documentation of the assessment of the LV function. If this has not been assessed, the CM can ask the floor nurse and the physician why it hasn't. After the discussion, the physician can order a test such as an echocardiogram to determine the LV function.

CASE MANAGEMENT AND ETHICAL ASPECTS

This holistic view can be overwhelming when the patient has very complex clinical, social, economical, and behavioral issues. The hospital CM has the challenge of looking at the situation from all angles and maintaining a nonjudgmental attitude. The CM must work with staff from all healthcare disciplines to achieve the best outcomes. This can be a challenge as ethical decisions come into play. The CM has to look at the situation holistically and consider what is best for the patient. This can become difficult when the payer says it will not continue to pay for the patient's current level of care but the patient is not ready for discharge. In addition, the family does not want to move the patient to a different level of care. This can occur when a patient's condition is terminal and the care can be given at a skilled nursing facility (SNF) or with hospice services. However, the patient also may not want to be discharged to a different level of care. The CM must know the resources available for the patient and collaborate with everyone involved. The CM must have the ability to communicate effectively with the patient and family and inform them of their available choices. In addition, the CM must have good communication skills when working with the payer to negotiate what is best for the patient.

IMPORTANCE OF CLINICAL KNOWLEDGE AND CASE MANAGEMENT

Not only must CMs have an excellent ability to work within a team and communicate effectively with staff from all healthcare disciplines, they must also have a strong clinical knowledge base. Without having this clinical wisdom, the CM cannot contest to a payer why a patient still needs to remain in the present clinical setting. For example, if the CM does not know the reason for certain medications, he or she may not be able to justify why a patient needs to continue an intravenous medication for the treatment instead of changing to an oral medication. Understanding the etiology of why treatments are given for certain conditions may help justify why a patient needs to continue the current treatment. In addition, the CM must be familiar with medication side effects and required monitoring to understand why the person needs to remain in the acute care setting. Although an SNF may give intravenous medications, this does not mean all intravenous medications are appropriate to administer in a skilled facility. For example, if a patient is receiving an IV antiarrhythmic drug, his cardiac status will need to be monitored. This is not something normally done in an SNF. If the patient's condition is not ready for a change to an oral antiarrhythmic medication, the patient will need to remain in the acute care setting. The CM's strong clinical knowledge is crucial for the role and understanding of why a patient needs to be in the acute care setting. In addition, the CM's sound knowledge helps portray a more credible image during discussions with physicians, patients, and families.

The CM must be resourceful, dependable, and able to work autonomously in some areas while working together in other areas. Although working independently and collaboratively may seem conflicting, the timing and situation determine which approach to use. When focusing on the patient's needs and discharge plan, it is crucial to work with the patient, physician, nurses, and staff from other healthcare disciplines. However, the CM should be able to coordinate and prioritize his or her work and caseload independently. The CM should be proactive and anticipate potential needs and issues before they arise. If the CM foresees an issue arising where the physician may need to intervene with the payer's physician, the CM should apprise the attending physician of the potential problem before a situation escalates. Then, if the attending physician must speak with the payer's physician, he or she is prepared.

TERMS FOR THE CASE MANAGER

The CM has the challenge of understanding various terms, such as the *prospective payment system*, *relative weights*, *complications*, *comorbid conditions*, *denials*, *appeals*, *benefits*, and *deductibles*, to name a few. To help understand these terms, the following basic descriptions are given. The *prospective payment system* is how Medicare pays acute care hospitals and SNFs depending on a predetermined rate. The *relative weight* (RW) is the predetermined number attached to each diagnosis-related group (DRG) that determines the payment for the resources potentially used for that DRG. Although the RW is different for every DRG, it remains the same for each specific DRG. For example, according to the Center for Medicare and Medicaid Services (CMS), the RW for DRG 195 is 0.7316 for every patient in this category, and the RW for DRG 178 is 1.4983 for every patient in this category (CMS, Table 5—List of MS-DRGs of the Federal Register, 2008). These are two different DRGs (195 and 178) with two different RWs (0.7316 and 1.4983) for each of these DRGs, respectively. All patients with DRG 178 will have one RW. All patients with DRG 195 will have another RW. Even though one patient may use more resources for the same DRG, the RW is predetermined and only potentially changes annually.

Complications and *comorbid conditions* (CCs) are additional diagnoses that require care, treatment, or monitoring other than the principal diagnosis. Some CCs may affect reimbursement depending whether the DRG is present on admission (POA) or a hospital-acquired condition (HAC) (see Chapter 3). A *complication* would be a condition that arises after admission, whereas a *comorbid condition* is something the patient already has. For example, if the patient is admitted with pneumonia and develops a urinary tract infection (UTI), the UTI would be a complication. However, if the patient has pneumonia and Parkinson's disease, the parkinsonism is considered a comorbid condition. The patient did not acquire this condition after admission; rather, it is a chronic condition.

A *denial* is when the payer has determined it will not pay for all or part of a patient's stay, services, care, or treatment. An *appeal* is the rebuttal process when the provider or designee requests the payment for the stay, care, or treatment to be covered even though the payer has initially denied the service. This appeal may be done in writing or verbally depending on the payer's process. There may be more than one level to the appeal process. In these cases, the patient's physician may need to communicate with the payer's physician or medical director to have the denial overturned. The *benefit* is the part of the covered services under the payer's health plan. The *deductible* is the amount the patient has to pay for his or her care or treatment before the payer will pay its portion of the bill. *Deductibles* and *benefits* vary with different payers such as Medicare, Medicaid, and insurances. This can be challenging for the CM because he or she has to know the payer sources and the requirements of each. Does the payer require a precertification for the hospitalization? What is the organization's precertification process? Because insurance payers may have different plans, the CM may need to contact the insurance provider to know what is covered under each plan. In addition, with the development of Medicare replacement plans comes even more diversity in the requirements and coverage. The array of payers' idiosyncrasies provides a challenge to the CM for getting the patients' services and hospital stays approved.

CASE MANAGEMENT AND THE ADMISSION PROCESS

The CM may be involved with the patient's case before the patient even enters the hospital doors. For the patient admitted directly from the physician's office, a simple telephone call to the admission staff can prepare the way for the admission. The physician's office may also notify the CM of a direct admission. The physician may have specific requests concerning the patient's situation that need assistance. This initial contact facilitates the CM's process in preparing the patient's case. Computer systems often can ease the flow as the patient's demographic information may be entered before admission. In addition, when the patient is admitted, his or her name may appear on the CM's work list, which allows the CM to be proactive and meet the patient before receiving a referral from a physician or nursing staff.

From the admission, the CM can examine the patient's record to determine if any obvious pieces of payer information are missing. Is the insurance or payer's identification number available? Is the effective date on the form? If the payer information is missing, a process should be established to obtain the information from the patient at the appropriate time. This may seem difficult when the patient is listed as "self-pay"; however, to not follow up can cause more dissatisfaction if the payer information is entered incorrectly and later the patient receives a large bill after discharge because no one addressed the issue while the patient was in the hospital. In addition, the patient may incur a precertification penalty because the wrong insurance was listed and the correct insurance company was not notified of the admission within the insurance's allowed period. Although one could say it is the patient's responsibility to notify the insurance company according to its policy, courtesy supports working with the patient when possible to facilitate the process.

CASE MANAGEMENT AND PHYSICIAN COLLABORATION

The CM and physician can collaborate to facilitate the patient's treatment and care in the hospital. The CM can help physicians by coordinating care and obtaining test results in a timely manner. This coordination can facilitate the care of the patient. For example, if a chest radiograph is done in the morning, the physician may have to wait until later that evening or the next morning for the report. Instead, if the chest radiograph is done at 8:00 AM, the CM can obtain the initial results from the radiology department, discuss the information with the unit nurse, and arrange for the information to be sent to the physician. From the results, the physician can adjust the treatment plan. He or she may adjust medications, order more diagnostic testing, or order another physician consult. If the CM calls the patient's insurance provider to get his or her stay approved, having the x-ray results and change in treatment plan can help get the stay approved. This is just one example of how the two disciplines can collaborate for efficient patient care. There are many situations in which the CM and physicians can work together to coordinate care. Because the healthcare world for physicians, nurses, and CMs may be hectic, coordination of patient care can help all involved, but most importantly the patient.

CASE MANAGEMENT AND ACCURATE DOCUMENTATION

The CM reviews the clinical record to determine whether the patient meets established criteria for admission. Does the patient's treatment and condition meet inpatient admission criteria? Although this may seem harsh, it is important to determine whether the patient meets criteria. If the person does not meet established criteria, the CM needs to speak with the physician. If the physician still believes the patient meets inpatient criteria, the physician should document the supporting information in the chart. This concept of documenting the accurate clinical picture is discussed in Chapter 4. The documentation should represent the clinical picture, and the clinical picture should be supported by accurate documentation. By reviewing the patient concurrently and discussing the case with the physician, the physician hears the CM's perspective of the criteria for meeting medical necessity. Then if a payer denial occurs, it should not be a surprise, and the supporting evidence should already be documented in the chart.

The CM and clinical documentation specialist (CDS) may have an intricate relationship as they both desire accuracy of documentation to support the clinical picture. Both review the clinical record to assess for a clearer picture of the patient's condition. Just as the CDS goes through a systematic review to examine the chart, the CM should do the same. This methodical approach can prevent missing key aspects of the patient's clinical condition while keeping the data organized.

THE DISCHARGE PLAN

The CM is not only interested in the patient meeting the admission criteria but also the discharge plan. The discharge plan should be addressed on admission. Even if the plan changes throughout the patient's stay, the day of discharge is not the time to initiate the plan. The coordination of care as the team works toward the discharge plan is a major area the CM and healthcare team can address through collaboration. A discharge planning checklist can facilitate the process. Will the patient be able to go home safely? Does the patient need short-term rehabilitation in an SNF or an acute rehabilitation setting? Does the patient need outpatient therapy? Does the patient need home healthcare? Is the patient's condition going to require a long-term acute hospital stay? Will the patient need a nursing home for long-term placement? Is the patient's condition terminal? Would the patient benefit from hospice? These are just some of the possible discharge plans.

Discharge Planning Checklist

Although not all the areas in the discharge planning checklist will apply, the discharge form gives a guide for potential areas to consider. See Figure 6.1. The CM should first assess what is the patient's previous living arrangement? Nursing home? Assisted living? House? Apartment?

• Patient's previous living arrangement________________________
• Reason for admission__________________________
• Comorbid conditions____________________________________
• New diagnoses____
• Support services/community resources______________________
• Supporting family or significant other_________________________
• Cognitive or physical deficits: new/old________________________
• Patient's discharge plan__________________________________
• Potential needs____
• Postacute transfer DRG_________________________________
• Educational needs______________________________________
• Medication needs_______________________________________
• Diet instructions/needs__________________________________
• Follow-up appointment scheduled with physician_________________
• Transportation____
• Communication with transitional setting________________________
1. Physician's office
2. Home healthcare
3. Nursing home
4. Skilled nursing unit
5. Acute rehabilitation
6. Long term acute care hospital
7. Hospice

FIGURE 6.1
Discharge planning checklist.

One story? Two story? What is the reason the patient was admitted to the hospital? Heart failure? Pneumonia? Exacerbation of a chronic condition? Does the patient have other chronic conditions that affect his or her ability to be discharged? This may be a mental or physical condition. Does the patient have a history of stroke with hemiparesis? Parkinson's disease? Dementia? What kind of services or resources did the patient have before being admitted? Home-delivered meals? Community care agencies? Home healthcare? Adult day care? Who provides support for the patient at home, such as cooking, cleaning, shopping, and laundry? Spouse? Son? Daughter? Neighbor? Local church group? What is the potential discharge plan? Home with the previous arrangement? Nursing home? Other new needs? What is the patient's current working DRG? Is this a postacute transfer DRG as discussed in Chapter 3? If so, how does this relate to the discharge plan? What are the patient's educational needs? Does the patient have a new condition on which he or she needs education? Or does the patient have an exacerbation of a chronic condition that the patient could use some educational reinforcement or updates? Are there changes in the patient's medications or diet about which the patient will need further education? At discharge, does the patient have a follow-up appointment to see his or her physician? This appointment can be scheduled before the patient leaves the facility. This not only helps the patient to have the appointment scheduled, but the office staff also knows when the patient has a follow-up appointment. While a patient may change the appointment, the initial step of scheduling the appointment has been completed before discharge. In addition, the CM needs to assess whether there are transportation needs. How will the patient get to the next level of care? Private vehicle? Wheelchair van? Ambulance? Has the CM communicated with the transitional setting, such as the physician's office or nursing home? This helps facilitate the transition to the next level of care so the receiving facility or entity has a more complete picture of the patient's situation. Although this checklist is not all-inclusive, it gives some guidance to areas the CM can address for the discharge plan (Figure 6.1).

Multidisciplinary Team and Discharge Planning

After reviewing the patient's clinical information and treatment plan, the CM speaks with the patient and physician to further assess the potential discharge plan and additional needs. One opportunity for the healthcare team is a multidisciplinary meeting to assess for enhanced coordination of care and discharge plans. This team may include the CM, physician, nursing staff, social services, dieticians, pharmacists, physical therapists, and occupational therapists. This collaborative approach allows the team to discuss the patient's case and care concurrently and assess for potential needs. Other disciplines may be involved, depending on the specifics of the case; however, when discussing a patient's case, the group must consider the patient's privacy and confidentiality.

READMISSIONS

Adequate discharge planning is particularly essential since readmissions into the hospital have become a focus of the CMS. According to an article by Jencks, Williams, and Coleman (2009), the 30-day hospital readmission rate for Medicare patients who had been discharged from the hospital was 19.6%. Moreover, approximately half of those medical patients did not have a documented bill for a follow-up physician office visit from the time they were released from the hospital and then readmitted. Another concern was the type of readmissions. According to this study by Jencks et al., heart failure and pneumonia were prevalent readmission diagnoses, especially for previous hospitalizations for medical conditions (2009).

Considering the various commonalities noted with readmissions, the CM has an opportunity to be part of the team to help decrease these rehospitalizations. Although patients' health conditions may deteriorate, requiring a readmission, developing a discharge process may help decrease these readmissions. The healthcare team can work together with the patient on assessing the patient's discharge plan as described previously using the discharge planning checklist. The multidisciplinary team can use the checklist as a guide to assess the patient's needs. See Figure 6.1. Although the list could be endless, these questions give the team a structured framework to assess the discharge plan.

Because readmissions and lack of patient follow-up physician appointments may have some correlation, ideally the team should set up the patient's follow-up physician appointment before the patient is discharged. This includes actually setting up this appointment in collaboration with the patient and physician's office (rather than only informing the patient of when he or she needs to make this appointment). In addition, because heart failure is one of the known readmission diagnoses according to Jencks et al. (2009), this provides another opportunity for discharge planning. When patients have a known history of chronic respiratory or cardiac diagnoses, they should be adequately assessed during the acute care stay for any potential exacerbations and educational needs. For example, if the patient has known CHF, is the patient's respiratory, fluid, and cardiac status stable? Has the patient received education on his or her medications, weight monitoring, and diet restrictions? If the patient has chronic obstructive pulmonary disease (COPD), has the patient been assessed for possible home oxygen? Does the patient understand his or her medications? Are there home factors that contribute to the exacerbation of the disease? Does the patient smoke or exposed to second-hand smoke? What are signs of a potential infectious process? Understanding the patient's disease process and instructing the patient on his or her condition and symptoms of changes in the condition can help the patient know when to notify the doctor before an exacerbation occurs.

CASE MANAGEMENT AND POSTDISCHARGE FOLLOW-UP

The CM can help coordinate the patient's stay and discharge process. Following up with the patient after hospital discharge allows the CM to monitor the patient's transition back into the community. Did the patient get his or her home medications filled? If the patient had home healthcare, did the agency come when scheduled? Did the patient have any questions or concerns he or she did not think of while still was in the hospital? Has the patient gone to the follow-up physician's appointment? Even if the patient went to another setting besides home, the CM can still contact the receiving facility to inquire whether the transition went as planned and any questions can be answered. This is also a time to confirm the exact discharge status with the receiving facility. The patient may have been scheduled to be placed into a nursing home's intermediate care bed; however, when the nursing home received the patient it assigned him to a skilled nursing bed. This is significant for the hospital's discharge status because it needs to match the status the patient went to. If the patient's diagnosis was a postacute transfer DRG (as described in Chapter 3) and the patient was admitted to an intermediate bed, the transfer DRG would not be affected. However, if the patient instead was admitted to a skilled nursing unit bed, the postacute transfer DRG policy would go into effect. The discharge status from the hospital should be updated to the correct status. This demonstrates how the CM can collaborate with the discharge facility to ensure this process is correct.

CASE MANAGEMENT AND DATA COLLECTION

Case management does not end with the patient's stay. Data collection can provide information to evaluate the case management process as trends and patterns are reviewed. Opportunities for improvement may be captured from this information. What is the readmission rate? Are there any trends with the readmissions? What is the period for the readmissions? Was the patient admitted with the same or similar diagnosis? Avoidable days or delays in services can be monitored using case management data. Was there a delay in tests or procedures? Was an appropriate transfer bed available for discharge? Monitoring these issues can help determine whether there are opportunities for additional collaboration, discharge planning needs, or process changes. Although data collection and trend monitoring can be overwhelming, understanding these areas and the interpretation of the trends can help the CM understand where he or she can make changes through collaboration.

SUMMARY

The CM is another member of the healthcare team who is vital in the collaborative process for patient care. The CM has the challenge of meshing the patient's clinical, psychological, and social information and discharge plan with the payer's requirements and the length of stay. The CM also is a patient advocate and may help with patient education. In addition, the CM has legal, quality, and ethical components to consider in his or her role. While the CM must know the above information, he or she must also have sound clinical knowledge. This strong knowledge base is essential when speaking with physicians and payers about the need for a patient to be at the appropriate level of care for his or her condition. In addition, proactive planning and excellent communication skills enhance the role.

The CM may be involved with the patient's care from admission to discharge. Even as the patient is admitted, the CM should consider the discharge plan and potential needs. A discharge planning checklist can help the CM work through this assessment and process. In addition, the CM should be part of a multidisciplinary team to assess the patient's needs. This team may include the CM, physician, nursing staff, social services personnel, dieticians, pharmacists, physical therapists, and occupational therapists. Not only can the CM help with the discharge process, but the CM also can help with the prevention of readmissions by scheduling follow-up physician appointments and assessing for signs of exacerbation of any chronic conditions before discharge. The CM is one more entity working together for the benefit of the patient.

REFERENCES

Centers for Medicare and Medicaid Services. 2008. Table 5—List of MS-DRGs, relative weighting factors, and geometric & arithmetic mean length of stay. FY 2009 final rule. *Federal Register* 73:161, August 19, 2008.

Jencks, S., M. Williams, and E. Coleman. 2009. Rehospitalizations among patients in the Medicare fee-for-service program. *New England Journal of Medicine* 360:14.

7

Putting It All Together

Although the clinical documentation specialist (CDS) can perform many functions that influence the financial and quality aspects of healthcare, the role should not encompass all these areas. The CDS role is not the same role as the case manager, the unit nurse, or the charge nurse. Rather, the CDS can support these positions by being the extra set of eyes during chart reviews, having collaborative discussions, and participating in educational opportunities. A CDS with a strong knowledge base and one who is accessible to staff and physicians provides an additional resource while the patient is still in the hospital. This real-time approach can benefit healthcare collaboration. Focusing on quality and timeliness of care can indirectly support the reimbursement aspect. The following scenarios will help us to further understand the application of this collaborative approach.

SCENARIO 1

While concurrently reviewing the chart of an 83-year-old male patient admitted to a medical nursing unit, the CDS notices the patient has an elevated BNP CHF, was dyspneic, and received IV furosemide. The CDS examines the clinical symptoms and treatment plan and queries the physician for supporting documentation of a diagnosis. In addition, the CDS notices the potassium level was 3.2 mEq (normal, 3.7–5.2 mEq/L) before the furosemide was given, and no potassium replacement or additional lab tests have been ordered (Medical Encyclopedia, n.d). The CDS notifies the patient's nurse of the lab result. Because an effect of furosemide is hypokalemia, the nurse is aware the potassium level may even be lower and notifies the physician (Rxlist.com, 2009). The physician orders repeat lab tests and a potassium supplement. During rounds, the physician documents hypokalemia and acute CHF. However, the CDS notices the last echocardiogram on the chart is from 8 years ago and the CHF is not documented as specifically as possible. The echocardiogram is used to evaluate the left ventricular function, which is also needed for a quality measure. The physician is made aware of the last echocardiogram and orders one for this hospitalization. Once the results are back, the physician documents acute systolic CHF, making the CHF diagnosis more specific.

SCENARIO 2

Another opportunity for collaboration is on the initial chart review. A 76-year-old woman is admitted from a nursing home with acute CHF. The patient is treated in the emergency room and then admitted to the hospital for further treatment and monitoring of her cardiovascular status. Although her initial lab results correspond with the CHF, the CDS also notes the other lab results in the chart. These lab results demonstrate an abnormal urinalysis with positive nitrites, increased white blood cells (WBC), and many bacteria. However, no urine culture was ordered. Discussion occurs with the physician, who orders a urine culture and sensitivity, which grows *Escherichia coli* bacteria, and the physician orders the appropriate antibiotic. The CDS sees on the admission assessment that the patient has a chronic indwelling catheter and foul-smelling urine. The CDS asks the physician for clarification of the etiology of the urinary tract infection (UTI) with the patient having a chronic catheter. The physician documents that the UTI is related to the chronic indwelling catheter and is present on admission. This not only supports an accurate picture of the condition, it also allows the coders to list the UTI as POA, and thus the UTI is not considered a hospital-acquired condition.

SCENARIO 3

Another example of teamwork is when the CDS reads in the nurse's admission assessment about a 54-year-old patient who has been treating a skin ulcer to his heel at home. The patient has chronic health conditions, including multiple sclerosis. The nurse documents the ulcer as Stage III (loss of full-thickness tissue but not exposing bone, muscle, or tendon as described by National Pressure Ulcer Advisory Panel, 2007). The patient's albumin is 1.7 (normal, 3.4–5.4 g/dL) (Medical Encyclopedia, n.d.). The body mass index (BMI) is 16.3 (normal adult range, 18.5–24.9) (Center for Disease Control and Prevention, n.d.). The physician documents that the patient has a heel ulcer on admission but does not specify the type. In addition, the CDS does not see a nutritional assessment from the dietician, and the patient is receiving a general diet. The patient's oral intake is only 40% overall for his first two meals. A team meeting occurs, and the CDS, nurse, dietician, case manager, and social worker discuss the patient's living arrangements, BMI, serum albumin, oral intake, and wound. A nutritional assessment is completed by the dietician, and recommendations are made for diet changes and a calorie count. The nurse requests a specific mattress and adds an intervention to the plan of care for a precise repositioning schedule. The social worker performs a home living assessment and discusses findings with the case manager, including the lack of social support and caregivers. The case manager discusses the nutritional status, wound, and living conditions with the physician, who orders skilled nursing for the discharge plan after speaking with the patient. The CDS writes two separate questions for the physician on the query form. One includes the clinical picture of the wound, specifically noting the nurse's assessment and stage of the wound along with the dressing care (treatment). The CDS is inquiring about further documentation of the type of wound. The second query focuses on the nutritional status of the patient, including the clinical picture of the low serum albumin and BMI, the 40% oral intake, and the patient's wound. The CDS is inquiring whether there is a corresponding diagnosis for this clinical picture. This type of collaboration demonstrates how different disciplines (CDS, dietician, nurse, social worker, case manager, and physician) put the clinical picture together to improve care and documentation.

SCENARIO 4

A 79-year-old woman is admitted from home with pneumonia. Reviewing the patient's chart, the CDS reads in the nurse's assessment that the "patient has difficulty with swallowing. The patient has a history of Parkinson's disease and reports an increased difficulty with ambulation." The chest radiograph is positive for pneumonia, and the WBC count is elevated at 16,000/μL (normal, 4,500–10,000 cells/μL) (Medical Encyclopedia, n.d.). The sputum culture grows gram-negative bacillus. The CDS queries the physician on the type of pneumonia, referencing the nurse's documentation of the "patient has difficulty with swallowing [and] has a history of Parkinson's disease," the sputum results, and the x-ray report of the pneumonia. The physician documents probable aspiration pneumonia and orders a swallow evaluation. The speech therapist performs the study and makes recommendations for a change in the patient's diet consistency along with swallowing techniques. In addition, with the progression of Parkinson's disease, the physician orders a physical therapy evaluation. At an interdisciplinary team meeting, the case management, social services, speech therapy, dietary, respiratory therapy, physical therapy, occupational therapy, and nursing staff discuss possible discharge needs. The patient is treated with appropriate antibiotics, oxygen, and nebulizers and is instructed on a mechanically adjusted diet and swallowing techniques. The patient improves and is able to be discharged home with home services.

SUMMARY

These scenarios are only minute examples of ways healthcare workers can collaborate. As rules and regulations change, it is vital for organizations to work together to understand the impacts of quality and finances and apply changes accordingly. This is not a one-person effort but rather a team approach. These scenarios can help one to understand how various disciplines can work together for the benefit of the patient in this complex world of healthcare.

REFERENCES

Centers for Disease Control and Prevention. n.d. It's not a diet, it's a life style—Body mass index. http://www.cdc.gov/nccdphp/dnpa/healthyweight/assessing/bmi/adult_BMI/english_bmi_calculator/results_normal.htm?pounds=120&inches=63 (accessed January 31, 2009).

Medical Encyclopedia. n.d. MedlinePlus. Potassium test. http://www.nlm.nih.gov/medlineplus/ency/article/003484.htm#Normal%20Values (accessed March 2, 2009).

Medical Encyclopedia, n.d. MedlinePlus. Serum albumin. http://www.nlm.nih.gov/medlineplus/ency/article/003480.htm (accessed January 31, 2009).

Medical Encyclopedia. n.d. MedlinePlus. WBC count. http://www.nlm.nih.gov/medlineplus/ency/article/003643.htm (accessed March 2, 2009).

National Pressure Ulcer Advisory Panel. 2007. Pressure ulcer stages revised by NPUAP. http://www.npuap.org/pr2.htm (accessed January 31, 2009).

Rxlist.com. 2009. Lasix (Furosemide) drug information: Uses, side effects, drug interactions, and warnings. http://www.rxlist.com/lasix-drug.htm (accessed January 15, 2009).

8

Final Thoughts

On a final note, when considering the various aspects of healthcare, one should make sure the right person is performing the right role. This is not just the person with the highest degree, most knowledge, or greatest experience. Nor is it necessarily the person who can apply clinical knowledge with excellent communication skills. These characteristics build the foundation of the position. However, the foundation's cornerstone must be passion. When a person enjoys the role, he or she radiates a positive attitude that may be contagious to coworkers. This lightens the setting of a potentially stressful environment. Happiness, humor, and contentment may be demonstrated with this behavior. However, enjoying one's job is not a learned quality. This comes from within and is vital for whatever job or position a person accepts. If this attribute is not present, the result is similar to placing a square peg into a round hole. One can try to adjust the parts that do not fit, but something is never completely right. Some part is cut short in the process, and both the square peg and round hole never really are suitable for the position. Putting the right person in the right position not only helps with the person's satisfaction of the role but also can support a positive behavior. Positive behaviors support collaboration. Moreover, successful collaboration can help promote safe, quality care.

Index

D

E

H

I

K

L

M

N

P

Author

Colleen Stukenberg has more than 20 years of nursing experience in a variety of areas. She has worked as a nurse in medical, surgical, orthopedic, and intensive care (ICU) units, as well as in a hospital-based skilled nursing facility (SNF) as a minimum data sets (MDS) care coordinator. In the MDS care coordinator role, she was knowledgeable in PPS (prospective payment system), RUGS, and long-term care regulations. She was involved with quality assurance and quality improvement in the SNF and the ICU settings.

Colleen's roles have also included work in health management as a case manager and professional development as a clinical development specialist (CDS). In the case management role, Colleen worked with a physician-based model where she would case-manage adult inpatients. In addition, she reviewed patients' charts and care for pay-for-performance and quality indicators, as well as accurate documentation. As a clinical development specialist, Colleen assisted with developing orientation plans for new employees and new graduate nurses.

In 2007, Colleen piloted a clinical documentation management professional (CDMP) position at FHN Memorial Hospital. Although the name is CDMP, it is based on accurate documentation as a CDS. With the success of the program, the CDMP role was made permanent, a position in which Colleen continues to work. As a CDMP, she has given educational presentations for physicians and nurses on accurate documentation, coding, present on admission, and recovery audit contractors.

Colleen's educational background includes two associate's degrees from Highland Community College, a bachelor's of science degree in nursing from Northern Illinois University, and a master's of science degree in nursing, specialization in health care education from the University of Phoenix.

Colleen is certified in medical surgical nursing and clinical documentation. In addition, she was inducted into Sigma Theta Tau International Honor Society of Nursing Beta Omega. She graduated from the University of Phoenix summa cum laude and is an advisory board member for the Association of Clinical Documentation Improvement Specialists.

Colleen lives in northern Illinois. She is married to Mike and has two boys, Ryan and Nathan. She enjoys watching the boys' school activities, reading, shopping, and going to church.